"Dunn's call for systemic reform in the field of historical Jesus research is a must read for anyone interested in understanding Jesus' significance and impact. Is it really possible to arrive at a credible, historical understanding of one who so quickly became the object of religious faith? Dunn says it is, but first we must ask why Jesus became the object of faith. By front-loading that question, Dunn turns the quest for the historical Jesus on its ear, providing new and potentially fruitful avenues for research. In this engaging book, Dunn maps out his plan in terms that are understandable, reasonable, and accessible to all who are concerned with the intersection of faith and history."

Mark Allan Powell, author of *Jesus as a Figure in History*

"After writing remarkable works on Christology and Paul, Dunn is turning his productive energies to the historical Jesus. In doing so, he must inevitably come to terms with contemporary research on the sayings of Jesus (Q)—in both moderate and exaggerated forms of that research—as well as with the results of the Jesus Seminar in California. In the process, Dunn has come to see that although the search for early, reliable, textually-transmitted material is preeminent in the construction of a portrait of Jesus, this material is liable to be misunderstood if the original context is ignored—namely, the context of a living tradition transmitted orally by disciples who had known Jesus even before the cross and Easter. Dunn's careful methodological exploration of the Gospel texts is thus also a contribution to the ecumenical reconciliation of Scripture-only and tradition-over-Scripture types of Christian believers."

Benedict T. Viviano, OP, University of Fribourg, Switzerland

Acadia Studies in Bible and Theology

Craig A. Evans and Lee Martin McDonald, General Editors

The last two decades have witnessed dramatic developments in biblical and theological study. Full-time academics can scarcely keep up with fresh discoveries, recently published primary texts, ongoing archaeological work, new exegetical proposals, experiments in methods and hermeneutics, and innovative theological syntheses. For students and nonspecialists, these developments are confusing and daunting. What has been needed is a series of succinct studies that assess these issues and present their findings in a way that students, pastors, laity, and nonspecialists will find accessible and rewarding. Acadia Studies in Bible and Theology, sponsored by Acadia Divinity College in Wolfville, Nova Scotia, and in conjunction with the college's Hayward Lectureship, constitutes such a series.

The Hayward Lectureship has brought to Acadia many distinguished scholars of Bible and theology, such as Sir Robin Barbour, John Bright, Leander Keck, Helmut Koester, Richard Longenecker, Martin Marty, Jaroslav Pelikan, Ian Rennie, James Sanders, and Eduard Schweizer. The Acadia Studies in Bible and Theology series reflects this rich heritage.

These studies are designed to guide readers through the ever more complicated maze of critical, interpretative, and theological discussion taking place today. But these studies are not introductory in nature; nor are they mere surveys. Authored by leading authorities in the field, the Acadia Studies in Bible and Theology series offers critical assessments of the major issues that the church faces in the twenty-first century. Readers will gain the requisite orientation and fresh understanding of the important issues that will enable them to take part meaningfully in discussion and debate.

A NEW PERSPECTIVE ON JESUS

WHAT *the* QUEST *for the* HISTORICAL JESUS MISSED

JAMES D. G. DUNN

Baker Academic
Grand Rapids, Michigan

Published by Baker Academic
a division of Baker Publishing Group
P.O. Box 6287, Grand Rapids, MI 49516-6287
www.bakeracademic.com

Printed in the United States of America

Library of Congress Cataloging-in-Publication Data
Dunn, James D. G., 1939–
    A new perspective on Jesus : what the quest for the historical Jesus missed / James D.G. Dunn.
        p.   cm.
    Includes bibliographical references and index.
    ISBN 0-8010-2710-1 (pbk.)
    1. Jesus Christ—Historicity—History of doctrines—20th century.
    2. Jesus Christ—History of doctrines—20th century. I. Title.
    BT303.2.D85 2005
    232.9′08—dc22   2004023187

CONTENTS

PREFACE

The following chapters represent a vintage matured over many years and often sampled during the maturing process to check that the process was properly under way. Different aspects under a variety of titles, usually variations on "Looking for Jesus," were delivered as lectures in San Antonio, Texas (1999); Uppsala (2002); Oxford (2002); and Hong Kong (2003); and as part of the Nils W. Lund Memorial Lectures, North Park Seminary, and Zarley Lectures, North Park University, Chicago (2000); the East Lecture, Lynchburg College, Virginia (2001); the Newell Lectures, Anderson University, Indiana (2002); the Thatcher Lecture, United Theological College, Sydney (2003); the Selwyn Lectures, St John's College, Auckland (2003); and the Dunning Lecture at the Ecumenical Institute of Theology, St. Mary's Seminary and University, Baltimore (2004). Simply running over these names again brings back many happy memories of good friends (old and new), of wonderful hospitality (often shared with Meta, my wife), and of interested and sometimes even enthusiastic audiences, students and others. The privilege of being granted some ability to teach and the joy of sharing insights with others, plus the stimulus of having to try to meet critical questions on points I count important and curious questions on points unexpected, made the experience wrapped up in these lectures a rich and rewarding one. I am more grateful than I can say to all who made these lecture trips possible and who gave so much of themselves to ensure that their guest(s) were as comfortable as possible.

These lectures all led up to the publication of my large-scale work *Jesus Remembered* (2003), the first volume, God willing, of a projected trilogy on *Christianity in the Making (27–150 CE)*. But I soon realized that what I regarded as the key methodological contributions made by *Jesus Remembered* might become lost in the scale on which I found it necessary to operate in the book. Fortunately, the invitation to deliver the Hayward Lectures, at Acadia University, Nova Scotia (November 2003), gave me the opportunity to spell out these insights more fully and to carry them further forward in the light of my continuing research. Meta and I are so grateful to our hosts, Craig Evans and Lee McDonald, for the original invitation and for the wonderful warmth of the hospitality afforded to us at Acadia.

In preparing the lectures for publication, it made sense to include the English-text version of my lecture at the Durham meeting of Studiorum Novi Testamenti Societas (August 2002), which appears as an appendix to the Hayward Lectures. The Greek-text version was published in *New Testament Studies* 49 (2003). The lecture is perhaps most accurately described as a prequel to *Jesus Remembered*, making the case in more detail than I could in the book for the need and importance for students of the Gospels to make a real effort to orient themselves to what must have been the oral character of the earliest traditions about and from Jesus. My last thanks are to Jim Kinney of Baker Academic for encouraging me to include this lecture in *A New Perspective on Jesus*.

February 2004

Abbreviations

BETL	Bibliotheca ephemeridum theologicarum lovaniensium
ExpTim	*Expository Times*
JSNTSup	Journal for the Study of the New Testament: Supplement Series
NovTSup	Novum Testamentum Supplements
NT	New Testament
RSV	Revised Standard Version
SNTSMS	Society for New Testament Studies Monograph Series
WBC	Word Biblical Commentary
WUNT	Wissenschaftliche Untersuchungen zum Neuen Testament

INTRODUCTION

Jesus was an epochal figure. For as long as human beings have curiosity about the past that helped shape them, Jesus will be a figure of fascination. He was, after all, the "founder" and focal point of the religion that has done more to shape Western culture than any other. So there will always be interest in what made him tick, what it was about him that attracted attention in the first place, why he was executed.

Christians have that interest redoubled tenfold or even a hundredfold. For them Jesus is the single most important man to have walked this earth. An orthodox belief that in and through this man God manifested himself as never before or since makes it inevitable that they will want to know as much as possible about this man. If God did indeed express himself through Jesus of Nazareth during his three (or whatever) years of mission, probably in the late 20s of the common era, predominantly in the relatively remote region of Lower Galilee, then it is of first importance to observe what he said and did during these years and in that context as clearly as possible. And if later reflection has elaborated (or obscured) the witness of Jesus himself, then it is proper to want to strip away that elaboration (or obscurity). It is Jesus himself the believer wants to encounter, not someone dressed up in robes borrowed from philosophy. If Jesus was indeed the incarnation of God, then what he said and did was presumably potent enough, and *any* secondary elaboration will simply detract from Jesus' own testimony.

Such has been the motivation behind what is commonly called "the quest of the historical Jesus." It has been primarily a scholarly quest, but expressive for the most part of the same restless curiosity and ardent desire to witness for oneself the reality of the historical phenomenon that motivates the sightseer or pilgrim of every age. The quest got under way as a serious scholarly pursuit more than two hundred years ago, and it has emptied many more inkwells than any other such historical inquiry. But it has also caused serious disquiet in many Christian circles less attuned to the scholarly methods and critical integrity of the questers.

My own conviction, which has grown steadily over the years, is that the quest as predominantly carried out over the last two centuries has been seriously flawed—and flawed from the outset in the perspective from which Jesus and the quest have been viewed. Quite proper concern to strip away later accretions has failed to distinguish the effect Jesus (must have) had from the subsequent evaluation of him. There has been too much looking back at Jesus through the lens of a long-established literary culture and too little appreciation of how the impact of Jesus would have made lasting effect in an oral society. The overall impression left by Jesus has been subjected to fine-detail critique and reconstruction without adequate appreciation of the extent to which that damaged the whole picture.

In the chapters that follow, I offer both a critique of these threefold failings and a new perspective on Jesus—a perspective that takes it as an axiomatic starting point that Jesus must have made a considerable impact on his disciples, which reflects on the way that impact will have come to expression in the earliest shared talk of the first disciple groups, and which attempts to focus primarily on the large picture and the overall impression that Jesus evidently left. If this endeavor helps to demonstrate the importance of asking such historical questions, as well as the dangers of some of the ways that have been pursued in seeking out answers to the questions, I will be well satisfied. And if my own attempted answers make sense to readers and help them to perceive Jesus of Nazareth more clearly for themselves, I will be highly delighted. But above all, my hope is, as with the larger book that these chapters in part summarize and in part carry forward, that the readers will begin to reexperience something of what the first disciples and churches experienced when they told again the stories about Jesus and reflected together on his teaching, and relived in turn the memories of Jesus' first followers. Now read on.

1

THE FIRST FAITH

*When Did Faith Become a Factor
in the Jesus Tradition?*

In my recently published *Jesus Remembered*,[1] I attempt to en-
gage with the long-running quest of the historical Jesus. I try
to highlight what seem to me the key issues, historical, herme-
neutical, theological, and the classic expositions of these issues.
I note what also seem to me important advances made in the
course of the quest, methodological insights that remain valid
to this day. But above all I hope that my own contribution will
itself constitute some advance in the quest—at three points in
particular. Elaboration of these three points will be the purpose
and content of the three chapters that follow. In each case it is
my contention that the earlier quests have failed because they
started from the wrong place, from the wrong assumptions, and
viewed the relevant data from the wrong perspective. In each

1. J. D. G. Dunn, *Christianity in the Making*, vol. 1, *Jesus Remembered* (Grand
Rapids: Eerdmans, 2003).

case they forgot what should have been more obvious than it evidently was and so lost the way almost from the beginning. First of all, they forgot the impact made by Jesus. The disciple-making, faith-creating impact of Jesus should be a fundamental given and an indispensable starting point for any quest for the Jesus from whom Christianity originated. It is this failure to appreciate and to evaluate properly the role of faith from the very first that is the focus of my first line of criticism of earlier quests. Not all questers, of course, are equally open to this criticism; it is the main thrust and consistent emphasis of the various quests with which I find fault.

The Christ of Faith versus the Historical Jesus

If the quest of the historical Jesus is characterized by one feature above all others, it is the contrast between "the historical Jesus" and "the Christ of faith," or probably more accurately, the *antithesis* between "the historical Jesus" and "the Christ of faith."

As is well known, the quest began by way of reaction against the Christ of Christian dogma. The Christ of the Chalcedonian creed, "perfect in Godhead and perfect in manhood, truly God and truly man," was just too unreal a human being. The Pantocrator, the world ruler, of Eastern iconography was too far removed from the man who walked the shores of the Sea of Galilee. How can we believe in such a Christ when, according to the Letter to the Hebrews, he was able "to sympathize with our weaknesses [and] . . . in every respect has been tempted as we are" (Heb. 4:15)? It is the human Jesus, the one who truly knew and experienced the reality of everyday existence in first-century Palestine, the Jesus who lived among the poor, who counted people like Martha and Mary as his close companions, who was known as "a friend of tax collectors and sinners" (Matt. 11:19), that we prefer to hear about. Is he not a more meaningful Savior than the almost mechanistic God-man or the remote Pantocrator? No wonder the cult of Mary, the mother of Christ, became so popular when her Son was so divine and so remote.[2] The

2. See, e.g., D. Brown, *Discipleship and Imagination: Christian Tradition and Truth* (Oxford: Oxford University Press, 2000), 250–53, 270–72.

heart yearning for comfort and an inspiring role model needed a mother figure to intercede with this awe-inspiring Christ, needed to rediscover the human Jesus behind the divine Christ.

The contrast between "the historical Jesus" and "the Christ of faith" initially came to prominence in the title of D. F. Strauss's slashing critique of F. D. E. Schleiermacher's *Life of Jesus*.[3] Schleiermacher's lectures had been given in 1832 and were already seriously behind the times\ when they were published thirty-two years later. In them he had concluded that the Fourth Gospel was written by John the son of Zebedee and therefore gave the most reliable and authoritative connected presentation of the life of Jesus. In the Fourth Gospel Schleiermacher found a Jesus who was the historical actualization of his conceptualization of religion in terms of the "feeling of absolute dependence." John's Gospel shows a Jesus who was distinguished from the rest of men by "the constant potency of his God-consciousness, which was a veritable existence of God in him."[4] "His consciousness of God never failed him, and apart from it he amounted to nothing."[5] In response, Strauss's critique was cutting. His opening words are ones of denunciation: "Schleiermacher's Christology is a last attempt to make the churchly Christ acceptable to the modern world. . . . Schleiermacher's Christ is as little a real man as is the Christ of the church. . . . The illusion . . . that Jesus could have been a man in the full sense and still as a single person stand above the whole of humanity, is the chain which still blocks the harbor of Christian theology against the open sea of rational science."[6] And his concluding sentences are equally bleak: "The ideal of the dogmatic Christ on the one hand and the historical Jesus of Nazareth on the other are separated forever."[7]

3. D. F. Strauss, *The Christ of Faith and the Jesus of History: A Critique of Schleiermacher's "Life of Jesus,"* Lives of Jesus Series (1865; ET: Philadelphia: Fortress, 1977); F. D. E. Schleiermacher, *The Life of Jesus* (1864; ET: Philadelphia: Fortress, 1975).

4. F. D. E. Schleiermacher, *The Christian Faith* (1821–22; 2nd ed., 1830; ET: Edinburgh: Clark, 1928), 12–18, 377–89; Schleiermacher, *Life of Jesus*, 88–104, 263–76.

5. Schleiermacher, *Life of Jesus*, 263.

6. Strauss, *Christ of Faith*, 4–5.

7. Ibid., 169.

The great goal of the first phase of the quest of the historical Jesus, then, was to get behind the Christ of faith in order to
recover the historical Jesus. The task was envisaged as though
it was equivalent to restoring a great masterpiece: the layers of
subsequent dogma were like the layers of varnish and dust ob-
scuring the authentic brush strokes of a Michelangelo; only by
stripping the layers of dogma away could the original authentic
genius of Jesus himself be uncovered. So the war cry arose:
back from the religion *about* Jesus to the religion *of* Jesus! Back
from the gospel about Jesus to the gospel of Jesus himself! The
task was to liberate the real Jesus, the historical Jesus, from the
chains and obscurations of later faith.

Not altogether surprisingly, given such a goal, two of the most
famous products of the liberal quest of Jesus uncovered a Jesus
who was a far cry from the Christ of dogma. In Ernest Renan's
romantic reconstruction, we find a Jesus who promoted "a pure
worship, a religion without priests and external observances,
resting entirely on the feelings of the heart, on the imitation of
God, on the direct relation of the conscience with the heavenly
Father."[8] And in Adolf Harnack's even more influential version,
we find a "historical Jesus" whose gospel centered on the fa-
therhood of God, the infinite value of the human soul, and the
importance of love. For Harnack, "true faith in Jesus is not a
matter of creedal orthodoxy but of doing as he did."[9]

By this time it was already clear that to recover the historical
Jesus was not simply a matter of stripping away the faith of creeds
and later dogma. *It was already the faith of the first Christians that
needed to be stripped away.* For Harnack, it was Paul who had
begun the process of transforming the simple Jewish moralizing
message of Jesus into the hellenizing religion of sacrificial cult.
Jesus' gospel focusing on the kingdom of God was transformed
by Paul into the gospel focused on Jesus himself.[10] By that time,
the end of the nineteenth century, Strauss's conclusion that in
the Fourth Gospel the Jesus of history had already been lost
behind the Christ of faith had become the standard consensus.

8. E. Renan, *The Life of Jesus* (1863; ET: London: Trübner, 1864), 87–88.
9. A. Harnack, *What Is Christianity?* (1900; ET: London: Williams & Norgate,
1901; 3rd ed., 1904); the final quotation is W. R. Matthews's summary in the 5th
edition (London: Benn, 1958), x.
10. Harnack, *What Is Christianity?* (3rd ed., 1904), 147, 180–81.

And William Wrede simply completed the circle by insisting that the Synoptic Gospels—not least the earliest of them, the Gospel of Mark—were also products of faith. "The messianic secret" of Mark, which holds the Gospel together, had been contrived in the process of composing Mark's life of Jesus.[11]

Wrede's conclusion proved to be of amazing influence and significance throughout the rest of the twentieth century; in the words of Norman Perrin, the *Wredestrasse* had become the *Hauptstrasse*.[12] It ensured that the Gospels, every one of the four canonical Gospels, would be regarded as *products of faith*. It ensured that the starting point for study of any Gospel passage would always be the assumption that the passage expressed the theology of that Gospel's author. To argue that the passage may afford an insight into Jesus' own understanding of his mission could never be assumed in the same way. The burden of proof always would lie with those who wanted to find here words that Jesus spoke or actions that Jesus took.[13]

This influence was soon reinforced by the development of form criticism. Form criticism began as an attempt to penetrate behind the written sources of the Gospels to uncover the earlier forms taken by the gospel story.[14] But the more influential aspect of form-critical method was the thesis that each unit of tradition must have had a life-setting, a *Sitz im Leben*, that explains and determined that form. The corollary was directly in line with the outworking of Wrede's thesis: the unit of tradition reflects most directly the concerns and faith of its setting in life, its *Sitz im Leben Kirche*.[15] If the reader wants to maintain that it (also)

11. W. Wrede, *The Messianic Secret* (1901; ET: Cambridge: Clarke, 1971).

12. N. Perrin, "The Wredestrasse Becomes the Hauptstrasse: Reflections on the Reprinting of the Dodd Festschrift," *Journal of Religion* 46 (1966): 296–300; cited by N. T. Wright, *Jesus and the Victory of God* (London: SPCK, 1996), 28.

13. N. Perrin, *Rediscovering the Teaching of Jesus* (London: SCM, 1967), 39: "The nature of the synoptic tradition is such that the burden of proof will be upon the claim to authenticity" (italicized in the original).

14. So explicitly in the opening words of both M. Dibelius, *From Tradition to Gospel* (1919; ET: London: Nicholson & Watson, 1934), v; and R. Bultmann, *The History of the Synoptic Tradition* (1921; 1931; ET: Oxford: Blackwell, 1963), 4; see also below, ch. 2 n13.

15. R. Bultmann, *Jesus and the Word* (1926; 2nd ed., 1934; ET: London: Nicholson & Watson, 1935), 12: "What the sources offer us first of all is the message of the early Christian community, which for the most part the church freely attributed to Jesus."

reflects a *Sitz im Leben Jesu*, that has to be argued for. However, it is the *Sitz im Leben Kirche* that can be taken for granted and that may have created the unit, or at least have greatly modified the tradition to make it speak to that setting. Consequently, there can never be any assurance as to how much or how little may go back to the setting of Jesus' own mission. The Christ of faith continues to obscure the historical Jesus.

Günther Bornkamm, in pleading the case for a new quest of the historical Jesus in the 1950s, well indicates how inhibiting such assumptions were. Almost immediately he observes: "We possess no single word of Jesus and no single story of Jesus, no matter how incontestably genuine they may be, which do not embody at the same time the confession of the believing congregation, or at least are embedded therein." He continues: "In every layer, therefore, and in each individual part, the tradition is witness of the reality of his history and the reality of his resurrection. Our task, then, is to seek the history *in* the Kerygma of the Gospels, and in this history to seek the Kerygma." "Nothing could be more mistaken than to trace the origin of the Gospels and the traditions collected therein to a historical interest apart from faith. . . . Rather these Gospels voice the confession: Jesus the Christ, the unity of the earthly Jesus and the Christ of faith."[16] So the Christ of faith pervades the Gospels, and pervades them so thoroughly that the quest of the historical Jesus easily loses itself in the mist of post-Easter kerygma and faith, which seeps from every nook and cranny of the Gospel story.

It is this total lack of confidence in our ability to penetrate fully through the layers of post-Easter faith that has undoubtedly been a major factor in persuading many scholars of the past and present generation to shift their attention away from historical questions regarding Jesus to reconstructing the context to which each Gospel bears witness. Each Gospel bears more immediate witness to the situation that gave it birth than to the originating impulse of Jesus' own mission. The debate about which traditions go back to Christ in, say, Mark's Gospel, has become lost in confusion, and our hearing has been deafened by competing views, so let us focus rather on what Mark's Gospel

16. G. Bornkamm, *Jesus of Nazareth* (1956; ET: London: Hodder & Stoughton, 1960), 14, 21, 23.

tells us about Mark's community and its social and cultural setting.[17] Or, why torture our congregations with the grim news that
we have so little confidence in our ability to hear and observe
through the Gospels what Jesus himself did and said? It is more
comfortable to bracket out questions of history and to focus on
the closed world of the narrative itself, where discussion can
be restricted within narrow and less threatening boundaries
and attention can be devoted to highlighting each evangelist's
storytelling genius.[18]

The latest round in the epic contest, the historical Jesus ver-
sus the Christ of faith, appears in the work of the Jesus Seminar. Robert Funk, the doyen of the Seminar, makes no secret
of his desire to rescue Jesus from Christianity; for Funk, the
continuing purpose of the quest of the historical Jesus "is to
set Jesus free from the scriptural . . . prisons in which we have
incarcerated him. . . . The pale, anaemic, iconic Jesus suffers by
comparison with the stark reality of the genuine article."[19] The
logic for this rescue effort is along predictable lines: whatever
can be attributed to the communities that used this tradition is
to be stripped away—any use or echo of Scripture; any saying
that is not aphoristic, parabolic, or a sharp retort; any hint of
baptismal practice or of the circumstances of the early Christian
mission; anything that smacks of common Israelite or Judean
lore or could have been said by any Christian sage; and particularly anything that is apocalyptic in character or hints at a
Paul-like theology of the cross; or in a word, any sniff of faith.[20]
Not altogether surprisingly, the Jesus who emerges for Funk is
"a free spirit," "a vagabond sage," "the subverter of the everyday
world around him,"[21] a historical reconstruction apparently all

17. For a good example, see H. C. Kee, *Community of the New Age: Studies
in Mark's Gospel* (London: SCM, 1977).

18. An early and influential example is D. Rhoads, "Narrative Criticism and
the Gospel of Mark," *Journal of the American Academy of Religion* 50 (1982):
411–34.

19. From the poster distributed in connection with Funk's lecture tour in
2000; the words are almost a quotation from R. W. Funk, *Honest to Jesus* (San
Francisco: HarperSanFrancisco, 1996), 300.

20. See, e.g., the references to the Jesus Seminar in the author index of Dunn,
Jesus Remembered, 959.

21.Funk, *Honest to Jesus*, 208, 212, 252.

the more convincing because it stands at such odds with the traditional picture of Jesus drawn from the Gospels. Funk's work and that of the Jesus Seminar are presumably intended to mark some kind of triumph of "the historical Jesus" over "the Christ of faith."

In all this a striking feature is readily apparent: that in the quest of the historical Jesus, faith is a hindrance, faith leads the searcher down the wrong road, faith prevents the searcher from recognizing the real Jesus. Faith is bad, history is good. The Christ of faith is what we need to get behind; the perspective of faith obscures and deceives; we will only attain to the Jesus of history when all the elaborations and distortions of faith have been stripped away, and when all faith has been eliminated from the record and the resulting picture. What started as a protest against the artificialness of the creedal Christ, what began as an attempt to strip away the centuries-old layers of dogmatic and ecclesiastical contrivance, has ended up as a rejection of the Gospels themselves and their portrayal of Jesus and a deep-seated suspicion of the Jesus tradition as a whole. It is all, from start to finish, the product of faith and therefore to be discounted.

It is this whole thrust that I find it necessary to question and challenge—on two grounds: first, we must recognize that the first faith of the disciples is what makes it possible for us to gain any information about or insight into the Jesus of Galilee; and second, we must also recognize the fallacy of thinking that the real Jesus must be a nonfaith Jesus, different from the Jesus of the Gospels.

The Impact of Jesus

An inescapable starting point for any quest for Jesus should be the historical fact that Jesus made a lasting impact on his disciples. It can be regarded as one of the most secure of historical a prioris that Jesus made a deep impression during his mission. No one with any sense of history can dispute that Jesus existed and that he was active in some sort of mission in Galilee, probably in the late 20s or early 30s of the first century, prior to his execution in Jerusalem "under Pontius Pilate." We know this because he left his mark on history. The historical fact of

Christianity is impossible to explain without the historical fact of Jesus of Nazareth and of the impression he left. What he said and did evidently "got home" to many people, and the impact that he made on them has resonated down through history.

In particular, he made disciples; the effect that he had on them in due course gave us the accounts of Jesus in the Gospels. The impact was not a slight one—a memorable epigram, a good story, or an exciting event that caught their attention for a day or two and then sank below the surface of their everyday consciousness. His mission changed their lives. They became disciples. They gave up their jobs. They left their families. They committed themselves to him, to follow him. They were in his company day after day for many months. The impact of his mission turned their lives in a completely new direction; it lasted.

The point I want to make here is that this response was already a *faith* commitment. They believed what he said; they responded to his challenge by joining his mission and trusting their lives to him; they believed in him. At this point it is not necessary to clarify what this faith consisted of or amounted to. The point is that the way they responded to Jesus can hardly be denied description with words like "faith," "trust," and "commitment." Jesus may have created many different impressions on different people, impressions that we can no longer recover. But in the case of the disciples, Jesus made a faith-creating impact, and it is from that initial disciple-making impact that all else follows.

This is the first point to be noted, then: faith among the disciples of Jesus did not first arise with Easter. Of course, that earlier faith was illuminated and transformed by what happened on the first Good Friday and Easter day. Of course, as Bornkamm observed, it is Easter faith that provides the context for all the traditions about Jesus in their present Gospel locations. The Gospels are clearly intended to preach the gospel. Each of them clearly is designed to build up to the climax of the death and resurrection of Jesus. But the disciples of Jesus did not first become disciples at the cross or on Easter day. They were already believers in Jesus prior to that; the faith was no doubt inadequate in the light of its subsequent fuller version, but it was still faith.

The second point follows. This initial faith shaped the Jesus tradition from the first. It would be possible to argue that the

impact made by Jesus was on individual disciples who treasured the memory of what they had heard Jesus say and seen
Jesus do; that they treasured that memory in their hearts and
only after Easter began to talk about what they remembered.
By so arguing some could continue to insist that the faith that
shaped the tradition from the first was Easter faith. It would
be possible, even, to argue that the individual disciples continued to treasure their memories of Jesus in the secret of their
hearts, and only when a Mark or a Matthew appeared, when
they were old, did they begin to feed these memories into the
newly developing tradition. That way we could be sure that the
Jesus tradition was first formulated from a perspective of well-
developed Christian faith.

But neither of these possibilities is even halfway plausible. It is
scarcely imaginable that what Jesus said and did was not talked
about. Gerd Theissen's *Shadow of the Galilean*[22] gives a good and
fair impression of the way accounts and rumors of Jesus' teaching
and action must have been widely circulated, readily available to
even the only faintly interested. And if stories were being told about
Jesus on a common interest basis, then it is highly probable that
those favorably impressed by Jesus would have had their own accounts of what it was that had impressed them, no doubt in part
at least to explain their interest in Jesus to skeptical or inquiring
neighbors. All the more so, then, should we expect those who had
committed themselves to Jesus' cause to talk about Jesus' teaching
and actions among themselves, not least to reassure themselves
that their commitment to Jesus had not been a mistake.

Such sharing of impressions, such reflecting on the striking
things Jesus had said, such retelling stories of Jesus' doings are
the obvious beginnings of the Jesus tradition. In this way, we
may say, the initial forms of the Jesus tradition first took shape.
The alternative, of disciples staying silent all during Jesus' mission, with no talk of what had most impressed them, with no
sayings of Jesus or memories of his healings to be shared when
there was nothing else to do of an evening—the alternative of
such hidden memories being suddenly jerked into verbal ut-
terance by the event of Easter is simply too incredible even to

22. G. Theissen, *The Shadow of the Galilean: The Quest of the Historical Jesus
in Narrative Form* (London: SCM, 1987).

be considered. Rather, it is a priori compelling to deduce that the Jesus tradition began as a matter of verbal formulation as the disciples talked together about the impact Jesus had made severally upon them.

Another way of expressing the same point is that such repetition of Jesus' teaching, such formulation of stories about what Jesus did, about his encounters with others, was itself an expression of the commitment they were already making to the cause of Jesus. I need to put the point quite bluntly. The earliest forms of the Jesus tradition were the inevitable expression of their faith in Jesus, the converse of their commitment to become part of his disciple band. I repeat, the first forms of the Jesus tradition were indeed the expression of faith—of disciple faith—not yet of Easter faith, not yet expressive of the gospel as it came to be expounded by Paul and the other first apostles, but nonetheless born of, imbued with, expressive of faith.

Fortunately this a priori deduction can be substantiated from the data of the Jesus tradition itself. In a very important but unduly neglected article, Heinz Schürmann demonstrated, by following form-critical principles, that the beginnings of the sayings tradition in the Gospels must lie in the pre-Easter circle of disciples, and thus, as he added, with Jesus himself.[23] The claim can be easily documented. Consider only the Sermon on the Mount (Matt. 5–7) or the parallel material in the Lukan Sermon on the Plain (Luke 6:17–49): the Beatitudes, the call to love the enemy and not retaliate, the demand to give to those who beg from you, the warning against judging others, about the speck in someone else's eye and the log in one's own, the tree known by its fruits, the parable of the wise man and foolish man. Which of these has been created and determined by the gospel of Good Friday and Easter? Which evangelist in the Pauline mold would have been content to indicate that future prosperity depended on hearing and doing Jesus' words, without any reference whatsoever to cross and resurrection? Much the more likely explanation is that such tradition was already treasured and formulated by

23. H. Schürmann, "Die vorösterlichen Anfänge der Logientradition: Versuch eines formgeschichtlichen Zugangs zum Leben Jesu," in *Der historische Jesus und der kerygmatische Christus*, ed. H. Ristow and K. Matthiae (Berlin: Evangelische Verlag, 1961), 342–70.

the disciples before Easter. The form given to the tradition had already become firm and established so that it was simply part of the pre-Easter Jesus tradition which the post-Easter churches took on board and continued to use. Of course, it was from then on recalled and used in a post-Easter context. But it was almost certainly already being used in that form in disciple gatherings before Easter. The faith that it expresses and that gave such tradition birth as tradition was the faith evoked by Jesus during his pre-Easter mission, disciple faith, not yet Easter faith, not yet Christian faith, but nonetheless faith in Jesus.

The importance of the point is well illustrated by the current discussion regarding the Q document, believed by most to be one of the sources, along with Mark, on which Matthew and Luke drew. In the current phase of the quest of the historical Jesus, as much attention is now being paid to Q as was paid to Mark one hundred years ago. Two features have been given especial prominence among those most active in Q research. One is the almost certain absence of a passion narrative from Q, which consists almost exclusively of sayings of Jesus.[24] The second is the Galilean character of the Q material: it appears to have been shaped in Galilee and to evince a Galilean perspective.[25] Added to this is the now fairly standard assumption that a Gospel reflects more clearly than anything else the community within which it originated or for which it was written—hence talk of a "Q community." In many discussions this quickly becomes the assumption that Q somehow *defines* this community; it held to this document over against other communities who are similarly defined by their document—Mark's community in particular.[26] Given such logic, the inference becomes fairly obvious: the Q community must be located in Galilee and must have espoused an understanding of Jesus at odds with or even opposed to the gospel of cross and resurrection presented by Mark. On this reconstruction, the Q community, rather like the old nineteenth-

24. This was one of the early conclusions regarding Q, which has remained largely beyond question for more than a century.

25. See particularly J. S. Kloppenborg Verbin, *Excavating Q: The History and Setting of the Sayings Gospel* (Minneapolis: Fortress, 2000), ch. 5; and the impressive argument of J. L. Reed, "The Sayings Source Q in Galilee," in *Archeology and the Galilean Jesus* (Harrisburg, PA: Trinity, 2000), 170–96.

26. Kloppenborg Verbin, *Excavating Q*, ch. 4.

century liberals, believed in Jesus as the great teacher of wisdom, the one whose pungent aphorisms and sharp retorts continued to be a subversive force within Galilee in the 40s and 50s.[27]

The logic behind this reconstruction is fallacious at almost every point. I have commented elsewhere on some of these fallacies, including what I call the "one document per community" fallacy.[28] Here I simply want to draw attention to the more obvious, much the more obvious explanation for the two features of Q that have been drawn into such speculation about the "Q community"—the absence of a passion narrative and the Galilean provenance of the Q material. The most obvious explanation for these features is that the Q material *first emerged in Galilee* and was given its lasting shape there *prior to Jesus' death* in Jerusalem. That is to say, it expresses the impact made by Jesus during his Galilean mission and before the shadow of the cross began to fall heavily upon either his mission or the memory of his teaching.

The whole line of logic, using Q to reconstruct the beliefs of a Q community, illustrates a curious trait in twentieth-century investigation of the Synoptic tradition. Here is tradition, Q, which purports to be tradition of Jesus' teaching, and which was evidently shaped in Galilee. Yet rather than draw the obvious conclusion, that this is the teaching of Jesus during his mission in Galilee, remembered and put into its present form by those who were with Jesus in Galilee, a quite different conclusion is drawn: that it reflects a post-Easter community of disciples who did not know about or were hostile to the message of Jesus' death and resurrection. Never mind that we know a good deal about Jesus' Galilean mission from non-Q tradition, and that the Q material is wholly consistent with that. Never mind that we know virtually nothing about churches in Galilee during the 40s and 50s. Never mind that the probability of Galileans not knowing or caring about what had happened to Jesus, his death in Jerusalem, must be almost zero. When scholarly argument continues to work with such assumptions, about faith corrupting tradition and about the priority of a form's *Sitz im Leben*,

27. Hence the importance of Q, in particular for the Jesus Seminar and for J. D. Crossan, *The Historical Jesus: The Life of a Mediterranean Jewish Peasant* (San Francisco: Harper, 1991).

28. Dunn, *Jesus Remembered*, 150–51.

without realizing that these assumptions should have been put in question long ago, no wonder its further logic demonstrates the negative proof of *reductio ad absurdum.*

In Q, in short, we see the evidence of the a priori argument mounted earlier. Q demonstrates that Jesus' teachings had not simply been remembered by his first disciples, but had been put into forms that reflected the local and temporal provenance in which they were delivered, and *had endured in that form.* The obvious deduction is that the teaching was put into these forms as an expression of the discipleship into which such teaching had called them—that is, to celebrate and share the mutual impact of that teaching, and to make possible further reflection on that teaching as the mission of Jesus and their discipleship developed. In other words, the Q tradition reflects and bears testimony to the faith-creating impact of Jesus' ministry. It was formulated as an expression of faith, indeed, but of the faith of the disciples that drew them into following him. As such, it takes us back not merely to the 70s or 80s when the Gospels were written, and not merely to the 40s, 50s, or 60s when the Jesus tradition was being circulated round the first churches, but to the late 20s or early 30s, to the time and mission of Jesus himself. As such, it enables us to hear, much more clearly than has regularly been assumed by Jesus researchers, Jesus himself as these first disciples heard him.

This brings us nicely to my second main complaint about the historical quest for the historical Jesus.

The So-Called Historical Jesus

A major problem with the quest of the historical Jesus is the very term "historical Jesus." It suffers from a split personality. On the one side, anyone who has attempted to define the meaning of the phrase is quite clear about it: "the historical Jesus" is the Jesus constructed by historical research.[29] This is important: on a strict and proper definition, "the historical Jesus" is not the

29. E.g., J. M. Robinson, *A New Quest of the Historical Jesus* (London: SCM, 1959), 26; J. P. Meier, *A Marginal Jew*, vol. 1, *The Roots of the Problem and the Person* (New York: Doubleday, 1991), 21–26.

man who walked the tracks and hills of Galilee; "the historical
Jesus" is what we know about that Jesus, what we can reconstruct of that Jesus by historical means. As Leander Keck puts
it, "The historical Jesus is the historian's Jesus, not a Kantian
Ding an sich (thing in itself)."[30] Despite that, however, on the
other side is the fact that "the historical Jesus" began life, as
we may say, by being set in antithesis to the Christ of faith. The
motivation behind the emergence of the phrase was a concern
to cut through the thickets of dogma to discover the real Jesus
behind them. Such motivation is not going to be satisfied if it
is met instead with the thickets of historical uncertainty; what
benefit is it to exchange the dogmatician's Jesus for the historian's
Jesus? In other words, the phrase itself, whatever the niceties
and qualifications of historical method, will not be satisfied to
be anything less than a reference to the flesh-and-blood man,
Jesus of Nazareth. And so we find, even among those who protest that they wish to stick with the first meaning, the Jesus
reconstructed by historical research, that "the historical Jesus"
is again and again being used for the man behind the Gospels,
the real Jesus, the actual Jesus.

However, such confusion only masked the real problem, the
fallacy that subverted the quest of the historical Jesus from the
first. This was the assumption that the historical Jesus must
be *different* from the faith-inspiring Jesus. Characteristic of the
quest is that it has been searching for a historical Jesus not simply behind but different from the Christ of faith, and different
not simply from the Christ of faith but in the end also different
from the Jesus of the Gospels. Of course, he must be different. It
was the nonhumanity of the Christ of faith that first motivated
the quest. It was the suspicion that Jesus of Nazareth has been
overlaid and hidden from us by post-Easter faith in Jesus as
Lord that has continued to drive forward the quest. So of course,
the human Jesus, the historical Jesus, must be different from a
Jesus seen through the colored spectacles of belief that Christ
was the divine Son of God. Let us by all means get back to the
human Jesus, the historical Jesus!

30. L. E. Keck, *A Future for the Historical Jesus* (Nashville: Abingdon,
1971), 20.

But the point already made undermines that whole project. For the point is that faith colors all the traditions we have about Jesus and has done so from the very first. Not Easter faith, as I have argued, but nonetheless faith. The earliest tradition bears witness in phrase and form to the impact made by Jesus. The formulation of that tradition was itself the expression of the trustful response that Jesus evoked from his disciples. The initial formulation of the tradition, we may say, was itself the impact made by Jesus. That which grasped and shaped their lives is what they put into verbal form in what we now call the Jesus tradition. And as we can tell the shape of the seal from the impression it makes on the page, so we can tell the shape of Jesus' mission from the indelible impression he left on the lives of his first disciples as attested by the teaching and memories of Jesus that they were already formulating during their initial discipleship. To quote Keck once more: "The perception of Jesus that he catalyzed is part of who Jesus was."[31]

There are two important corollaries to this insight. One is that we can never succeed in stripping away that faith from the tradition, as though to leave a nonfaith core. When we strip away faith, we strip away everything and leave nothing. We cannot press back through the tradition to a Jesus who did not make an impression, or a Jesus who might have made a different impression. All we have is the impression actually made. And all we can deduce from that is the character and teaching of the mission that produced that impression. This is precisely why I called my book *Jesus Remembered*—because we have access to none other than to *Jesus as he was remembered*. The historical Jesus at best can be none other than the Jesus-who-made-the-impact-which-is-the-beginning-of-the-Jesus-tradition. We can see Jesus of Nazareth only through the eyes and ears of these first disciples, only through the impressions embodied in the teaching and stories of Jesus that they put into their enduring forms.

The attempt to understand and perform historical research on the model of scientific research, or latterly on the model of

31. L. E. Keck, *Who Is Jesus? History in Perfect Tense*, Studies on Personalities of the New Testament (Columbia: University of South Carolina Press, 2000), 20.

archaeological research, has simply compounded the misunder-
standing. The quest of the historical Jesus has been conducted as
though it were like Madame Curie's quest for radium, a process
of filtering out all other elements until the final precipitate, the
long sought for element itself was exposed to view. Or like the
archaeologist digging down through layers of historical strata
in the hope of uncovering some artifact in the earliest stratum
that might explain why so much happened subsequently on that
site. As though "the historical Jesus" were a hidden element, an
archaeological artifact, a something, a *Ding an sich*, that could be
brought to sight and viewed wholly afresh, wholly independently
of anything said about him then or thereafter. But that was never
more than fanciful. The only Jesus available to us, I repeat, is
*Jesus as he was seen and heard by those who first formulated the
traditions we have*—the Jesus of faith, Jesus seen through the
eyes and heard through the ears of the faith that he evoked by
what he said and did.

The other corollary is that we really do not have any other
sources that provide an alternative view of Jesus or that com-
mand the same respect as the Synoptic Gospels in providing
testimony of the initial impact made by Jesus. We do not have
an independent record of Caiaphas's view of Jesus or of Pilate's
judgment regarding Jesus; that is, no sources that attest a nonfaith or a hostile response to Jesus. Would that we had; it would
at least have enabled some triangulation between quite different
reference points. And other mentions of Jesus in nondisciple
sources are too allusive to help us much.[32] It is true that several
scholars, mainly associated with the Jesus Seminar, but also
others, want to argue that some of the later gospels, notably the
Gospel of Thomas, provide evidence of a different faith response
to Jesus. But while *Thomas* does indeed contain versions of
Jesus' teaching, some of which are early in formulation, it is the
Synoptic tradition that provides the yardstick by which such
judgments (early or late) can be made. And the modest enrich-
ment of our knowledge of early tradition that *Thomas* offers, in
the event, attests the same sort of impact made by Jesus as we
find, in particular, in the Q tradition. Nevertheless, the distinctive *Thomas* material in almost every case probably attests the

32. Reviewed briefly in Dunn, *Jesus Remembered*, 141–42.

influence of later faith, gnostic faith. In that respect, we may say, the *Gospel of Thomas* is like the Gospel of John: they both attest the influence of later faith, in the one case gnostic faith, in the other Christian faith; that is, both exemplify in their different ways the Christ of faith in protest against which the quest of the historical Jesus was first undertaken.[33]

Once again, then, we are confronted with the, to some, uncomfortable fact that the only Jesus we can hope to find in any quest is *the Jesus of the Gospels*, that is, the Jesus who made the impact which was the first phase of the Jesus tradition, but which also gave so much of the Jesus tradition the lasting form still preserved for us in the Synoptic Gospels. And is not this the Jesus we want to recover—the Jesus who made the impact thus embodied in the Gospels? The Jesus we are seeking is not some Jesus who might or might not have been significant, or who might or might not be more meaningful to nineteenth-century liberalism or to twentieth-century modernism or to twenty-first-century postmodernism. That Jesus is a will-o'-the-wisp who draws questers unwittingly into the swampy ground of arguments of infinite regression. In contrast, the Jesus we want to find is the Jesus who *was* significant, the Jesus who made the impact he did, the Jesus who was the fountainhead from which Christianity flowed, the Jesus who transformed fishermen and toll collectors into disciples and apostles. My point is simply that by recognizing the impact that Jesus made, as attested by the Jesus tradition, we can still hope to experience something of that impact today.

Those of you familiar with the history of the quest will be well aware that I am mounting an argument similar to that pressed home more than one hundred years ago by Martin Kähler in his well-known essay *The So-Called Historical Jesus and the Historic Biblical Christ*.[34] Kähler's point was that we have no sources capable of sustaining a biography of Jesus. The Gospels are inadequate as sources for a life of Jesus. Consequently, biographers of

33. See again and further in ibid., 161–71.
34. M. Kähler, *The So-Called Historical Jesus and the Historic Biblical Christ* (1892; ET: Philadelphia: Fortress, 1964). L. T. Johnson, *The Real Jesus* (San Francisco: HarperSanFrancisco, 1996), mounts the equivalent attack on the neoliberalism of the Jesus Seminar.

Jesus can achieve their goal only by drawing upon what Kähler called a fifth gospel, meaning the historian's own ideals. They fill up the gaps in the Gospel record read as history by reading into the accounts elements of their own faith and priorities. Hence "the so called historical Jesus." The many and varied Jesuses of the nineteenth-century quest were the result of the many and varied ideals and principles drawn upon to fill out the scant and uncertain historical data of the Gospels themselves—hardly deserving the title "historical" in the proper sense. In complete contrast, argued Kähler, what we have in the Gospels is "the historic biblical Christ." The two words translated "historical" and "historic" (*historische* and *geschichtliche*) make his point. *Historie* he understands as merely historical, the bare data, independent of any significance that might be placed on them. *Geschichte*, on the other hand, denotes history in its significance, historical events and persons that attract attention by reason of the influence they have exercised. The point is that the Gospels present the *geschichtliche Christus*, Jesus seen in his significance. Yet we see the contrasting attempt to uncover a historical Jesus, stripped of the significance hitherto attributed to him, and now rather like a bare tailor's dummy ready to be clothed with the significance modern individuals might claim to see in him or choose to clothe him with—a ludicrous nonsense.

The point is obviously similar to the one argued above: that there is no historical Jesus to be found in the Gospels, only the historic figure evident to us through the influence he exercised on his disciples, through the impact he made on them in calling them into discipleship. The difference is that Kähler thought in terms of "the biblical Christ," the Christ who was preached by the early Christians. In other words, he was thinking in terms of what later would be understood as post-Easter faith. It was in such terms that Bultmann owned the influence of Kähler: what stood at the center for Bultmann was the kerygma, the kerygmatic Christ, the preached Christ.[35] But my reformulation of Kähler's point in terms of the *first* faith, the *pre*-Easter faith of the disciples, still recognizes the force of Kähler's argument without following Bultmann in discounting all faith other than

35. Most famously in R. Bultmann, "New Testament and Mythology" (1941), in *Kerygma and Myth*, ed. H. W. Bartsch (ET: London: SPCK, 1957), 1–44.

Easter faith. Thus reformulated, Kähler's argument is even more effective. To discount the influence that Jesus actually had, to strip away the impact that Jesus actually made, is to strip away everything and to leave an empty stage waiting to be filled by some creative amalgam of the historian's own imagination and values. If we are unsatisfied with the Jesus of the Synoptic tradition, then we will simply have to lump it; there is no other truly historical or historic Jesus. Only the Jesus whom we can see and hear through the influence he had, through the impact he made on his first disciples, as evidenced by the traditions that they formulated and recalled, only that Jesus is available to the quester. But, and this is my point, this Jesus *is* available to the quester.

To conclude. Thus far I have made only these two points of protest against the mainstream of the quest of the historical Jesus. First, it has failed to recognize that the faith-creating impact Jesus made on those he called into discipleship is the appropriate and indeed the most obvious and necessary starting point for any attempt to "get back" to Jesus. It has failed to recognize that the Jesus tradition is the direct effect of that impact, expressive of its force and character, and clear testimony of that impact. And second, the quest has been too long captivated by the will-o'-the-wisp of a historical Jesus, an objective artifactual figure buried in the Gospels and waiting to be exhumed and brandished aloft, as different from the Jesus of the Gospels—not fully realizing that the less the reconstructed Jesus owed to the Synoptic picture of Jesus, the more it must be expressive of the agendas of the individual questers.

These are the only two points I want to make here and now. There is more to be said, and my criticisms of the earlier phases of the quest are incomplete. But the fuller critique requires a further two chapters.

2

Behind the Gospels

What It Meant to Remember Jesus
in the Earliest Days

One of the most striking flaws in the quest of the historical Jesus results from the fact that it was undertaken in the age of the printed word. Gutenberg and Caxton[1] had instituted a revolution in human perspective in sixteenth-century Europe much more significant in its outworkings than the revolution associated with the names of Copernicus and Galileo. For two centuries the literary mind-set had been forming—the assumption, the taken-for-granted presupposition that written text is the only way in which important words can be preserved and passed on. Of course, there were still great orators, like Gladstone or Spurgeon, but their speeches and sermons, no matter how moving in the hour of hearing, could only successfully be "caught" and heard by others through their publication and circulation in written form. Consequently, we in the West simply take it for granted that the basis of a sound education is the ability to read

1. William Caxton (ca. 1422–91) was the first English printer.

and write. And when we today think of teaching and learning about the past, we think in terms of books and learned essays. A library is the natural habitat of the historian. In a word, we are all children of Gutenberg. Our way of conceptualizing the accurate transmission of information is determined by the *literary paradigm*.

All this means that we have little or no idea what it would have been like to live in an *oral* culture. But first-century Palestine certainly was an oral rather than a literary culture. Those who have inquired most closely into the subject tell us that literacy in Palestine at the time of Jesus would probably have been less than 10 percent.[2] There are grounds for questioning that figure, given the importance of Torah learning in Jewish culture. But given equally that royal officials, priests, scribes, and Pharisees would have made up the major portion of the small literary minority, the corollaries are probably much the same. These corollaries include the fact that knowledge of Torah for most people would have been by *hearing*, aural, rather than by reading.[3] We have to assume, therefore, that the great majority of Jesus' first disciples would have been functionally illiterate. That Jesus himself was literate cannot simply be assumed.[4] And even allowing for the possibility that one or two of Jesus' immediate disciples were able to read and write (Matthew) and may even have kept notes of Jesus' teaching, it remains *overwhelmingly probable that the earliest transmission of the Jesus tradition was by word of mouth*.

The point of all this for the quest of the historical Jesus, of course, is that our only way through to Jesus of Nazareth, if at all, is through the Jesus tradition, the tradition of what Jesus said and did, the Synoptic tradition in particular. The second main theme of my critique of earlier phases of the quest, then,

2. Recent estimates are of less than 10 percent literacy in the Roman Empire under the principate, falling to perhaps as low as 3 percent literacy in Roman Palestine; see below, 90n34.

3. Cf. Jesus' reported challenge to Pharisees, "Have you not read?" (Mark 2:25; Matt. 12:5; 19:4) with his challenge to the disciples, "You have heard" (Matt. 5:21, 27, 33, 38, 43).

4. J. D. Crossan, *The Birth of Christianity* (San Francisco: HarperSanFrancisco, 1998), 235, has little doubt that Jesus was illiterate. Luke 4:16–30 is usually regarded as a Lukan elaboration of the briefer tradition in Mark 6:1–6.

once again has two sides: first, the failure of earlier questers to appreciate how incapable the literary mind-set is to appreciate the way in which the Jesus tradition came to be formulated in the first place; and second, the failure to take seriously and to make sustained inquiry into what transmission of such tradition would have involved in first-century Palestine.

The Inadequacy of the Literary Paradigm

Anyone who is familiar with the two-century-old attempt to use the Gospels as sources for information about Jesus will need no reminding of how dominant the literary paradigm has been. It was concern to know about the historical Jesus, the real Jesus, that drove forward the debate about the sources for the Synoptic Gospels, the Synoptic Problem, as it has usually been known. The assumption was, of course, that the earlier the source, the more reliable would be the information it contained about Jesus. But although the role of oral traditions in the process featured in some early stages of the discussion,[5] the solution that came to dominate both Gospel research and life-of-Jesus research from the late nineteenth century onward was the two-source theory, or two-document hypothesis—Mark as the earliest of the Synoptic Gospels, a source for Matthew and Luke together with the sayings source Q—both, of course, *written* documents.[6] And even when some variations were offered in explanation of some of the complexities of the data, like *Ur-Markus* or Proto-Luke, what was envisaged were still *written* documents.[7] Researchers similarly regarded the special additional sources on which Matthew and Luke may have drawn, M and L, as written. In the

5. See further the brief treatment in my "Altering the Default Setting: Re-envisaging the Early Transmission of the Jesus Tradition," *New Testament Studies* 49 (2003): 139–75 (reprinted as an appendix to the present work), on which I draw extensively in parts of this chapter.

6. See, e.g., W. G. Kümmel, *The New Testament: The History of the Investigation of Its Problems* (ET: Nashville: Abingdon, 1972), 146–51; Kloppenborg Verbin, *Excavating Q*, 295–309.

7. On *Ur-Markus*, see, e.g., W. G. Kümmel, *Introduction to the New Testament* (ET: Nashville: Abingdon, 1975), 61–63; and on Proto-Luke, particularly, see V. Taylor, *Behind the Third Gospel* (Oxford: Clarendon, 1926).

English-speaking world B. H. Streeter provided the most authoritative and influential resolution of the Synoptic Problem. In it he
certainly recognized the importance of "a living oral tradition"
behind the Gospels and indeed cautioned against studying the
Synoptic Problem "merely as a problem of literary criticism."
Likewise, he fully recognized the need to look beyond the two
sources of Mark and Q to explain the composition of the Synoptic Gospels. Ironically, however, it was he who is particularly
recalled for his promotion of "a four *document* hypothesis."[8] The
literary paradigm continued to determine the way the problem
and its solution were conceptualized.

The main alternatives offered to the dominant two-document
hypothesis have been those of William Farmer[9] and Michael
Goulder.[10] Farmer argues against Markan priority and for the
traditional view that Matthew was the earliest written Gospel. He
maintains that the best explanation for the substantial parallels
between the three Synoptic Gospels is that Luke copied from
Matthew and that Mark copied from both Matthew and Luke. For
us *copied* is the key word—the relationships between the Synoptic Gospels conceived in exclusively literary terms. The possibility
that a later evangelist knew differing oral forms of the tradition
used by the earlier Gospel writer does not even enter into the
field of possibilities. Goulder argues differently: that Mark was
indeed first, but that Matthew was derived entirely from Mark,
and Luke from a combination of the first two—eliminating the
need for the Q hypothesis. Even substantial literary redaction
is regarded as a more plausible hypothesis than that Matthew
and Luke were aware of tradition apart from Mark, oral Jesus
tradition. And Mark Goodacre, Goulder's chief disciple, despite
acknowledging the potential importance of oral tradition, when
he turns to individual cases he thinks it sufficient to discuss them
in terms exclusively of literary dependence.[11]

8. B. H. Streeter, *The Four Gospels: A Study of Origins* (London: Macmillan,
1924), ch. 9 (quotations from 229).

9. W. Farmer, *The Synoptic Problem* (New York: Macmillan, 1964).

10. M. Goulder, *Luke: A New Paradigm*, 2 vols., JSNTSup 20 (Sheffield: Sheffield Academic Press, 1989), in his attempt to dispense with Q (particularly vol.
1, ch. 2).

11. M. Goodacre, *The Case against Q* (Harrisburg, PA: Trinity, 2002), 56–59,
89–90 (despite 64–66, 188).

The main development from and challenge to *source* criticism was, of course, *form* criticism, which began as a deliberate attempt to break away from the literary paradigm to conceptualize the transmission process in oral terms. The character of this oral tradition had already been identified by Julius Wellhausen in his analysis of the Synoptic Gospels: "The ultimate source of the Gospels is oral tradition, but this contains only scattered material";[12] the Jesus tradition as oral tradition was known only in small units. Bultmann took up the challenge when he defined the purpose of form criticism thus: "to study the history of the oral tradition behind the gospels."[13] Unfortunately, however, Bultmann could not escape from the literary mind-set, his own literary default setting; he could not conceive of the process of transmission except in literary terms. This becomes most evident in his conceptualization of the whole tradition about Jesus as "composed of a series of layers."[14] The imagined process is one where each layer is laid or builds upon another. Bultmann made such play with it because, apart from anything else, he was confident that he could strip off later (Hellenistic) layers to expose the earlier (Palestinian) layers.[15] The image itself, however, is drawn from the literary process of editing, where each successive edition (layer) is an edited version (for Bultmann, an elaborated and expanded version) of the previous edition (layer). But is such a conceptualization really appropriate to a process of *oral* retellings of traditional material? Bultmann never really addressed the question, despite its obvious relevance. He simply assumed that the transmission of oral tradition was no different in character from the transmission of already written tradition.

The most recent discussions of the history of the Synoptic tradition (to use the title of Bultmann's famous work) mark no significant change. As already noted, the main focus of attention has become Q, the second source apart from Mark in the two-

12. J. Wellhausen, *Einleitung in die drei ersten Evangelien* (Berlin: Georg Reimer, 1905), 43.
13. R. Bultmann (with K. Kundsin), *Form Criticism* (1934; ET: New York: Harper Torchbook, 1962), 1.
14. R. Bultmann, *Jesus and the Word* (1926; ET: New York: Scribners, 1935), 12–13.
15. Ibid.

source hypothesis. That Q was a document, written in Greek, has become one of the principal points of consensus,[16] although over-dependence on the literary paradigm again dictates, as with Mark and *Ur-Markus*, that divergences between Matthean and Lukan Q material have to be explained by postulating different versions of Q, a Q^{Mt} and a Q^{Lk}.[17] The debate, however, now focuses on the issue whether different compositional layers can be distinguished *within* Q, with John Kloppenborg's hypothesis that three layers can be so discerned winning a substantial following.[18] What is of interest here is the almost explicit assumption that *each layer is to be conceived as a written document*, and the process of development conceived in terms of editing and redaction. It should occasion no surprise that Kloppenborg envisages his investigation of Q in terms of an archaeological dig, as *Excavating Q*, where, as with Bultmann, the process is visualized as stripping away successive layers to reach the bottom layer, or as removing the redactional elements of successive editions to recover the original edition.[19] The literary paradigm evidently brooks no alternative.

Perhaps the clearest signal of the way the literary mind-set configures the whole problem in conceptualizing the history of the Jesus tradition is the weight of significance invested in the literary character of the Jesus tradition. One or two voices even question whether there ever was a period of oral tradition in the first place.[20] The possibility that some of the first disciples had scribal skills and could already have recorded, albeit in note form, the words and deeds of Jesus as earwitnesses and eyewitnesses is regarded as a major "plus" in favor of the reliability

16. See particularly C. M. Tuckett, *Q and the History of Early Christianity* (Edinburgh: Clark, 1996), ch. 1; Kloppenborg Verbin, *Excavating Q*, 87–111.

17. E.g., U. Schnelle, *The History and Theology of the New Testament Writings* (ET: London: SCM, 1998), 187.

18. J. S. Kloppenborg, *The Formation of Q: Trajectories in Ancient Wisdom Collections* (Philadelphia: Fortress, 1987).

19. Kloppenborg does not explicitly address the issue of whether Q^1 was also a document, but he does assume it (*Excavating Q*, 159, 197, 200, 208–9); see also 154–59 on the genre of Q^1.

20. W. Schmithals, "Vom Ursprung der synoptischen Tradition," *Zeitschrift für Theologie und Kirche* 94 (1997): 288–316, continues to argue that the Synoptic tradition was literary from the first. E. E. Ellis, *Christ and the Future in New Testament History*, NovTSup 97 (Leiden: Brill, 2000), 13–14, also queries whether there was an initial oral stage of transmission.

of the tradition.[21] And Barry Henaut argues strenuously that it is virtually impossible to recover any oral tradition behind the Gospels: oral tradition was wholly fluid and contingent on the particularities of each performance; all differences, no matter how great, can be explained in terms of literary redaction.[22] Such a view is typical across the board among those working with the Gospel tradition: if the content, character, and placement of the individual item of tradition can be explained in its present context, then no more need be said; it has been explained.

In all this the value invested in the Jesus tradition as *written* becomes dangerously and even frighteningly excessive. Most recognize that there must have been a period in which the memories and accounts of Jesus' mission circulated in oral form, perhaps for a period of twenty years or so before substantial written versions of these traditions began to appear. But they can conceptualize the process of transmission only as written tradition, as the process of copying and editing earlier written material. If then we have to acknowledge a gap of about twenty years before we can begin to understand that process, then we have *a gap between Jesus and the written tradition that we cannot hope to bridge.* And if we regard only written tradition as reliable and cannot conceive of oral transmission through time and space as anything other than unreliable, then *we have to despair of ever bridging that gap.* The oral period of the Jesus tradition, say 30–50 CE, becomes a great gulf fixed between the historian of tradition and Jesus of Nazareth that no person can cross. No wonder, then, that such attempts as have been made to venture behind the earliest written sources have been so contested and have won so little support within the guild of critical scholarship. For all such attempts are fated to fall into the gulf of the oral tradition period; or to use an alternative metaphor, they have been caught in the bottomless swamp of disputed claims regarding this saying and that story. And all this because our onboard computer has a literary default setting, so that we can

21. See particularly A. Millard, *Reading and Writing in the Time of Jesus,* Biblical Seminar 69 (Sheffield: Sheffield Academic Press, 2000), 223–29; also E. E. Ellis, *The Making of the New Testament Documents* (Leiden: Brill, 1999), 24, 32, 352.
22. B. W. Henaut, *Oral Tradition and the Gospels: The Problem of Mark 4,* JSNTSup 82 (Sheffield: JSOT, 1993).

only conceptualize the Jesus tradition in terms of a literary process and evaluate its usefulness and reliability accordingly.

This, I suggest to you, is the second major flaw in the quest of the historical Jesus: an ability to envisage the transmission of the Jesus tradition tightly constricted by the literary paradigm inbred in us; an unwillingness to take seriously the question whether oral tradition would have functioned like literary tradition; a negative evaluation of oral tradition as to its reliability as testimony to Jesus; and consequently a negative judgment as to the questers' ability to say anything with much confidence about Jesus.

Is it possible to redress such a serious imbalance in perspective and procedure? I believe so.

Attempts to Re-envisage Oral Tradition

Can we say more about the character of oral tradition and about oral transmission? As E. P. Sanders points out, the problem is "that we do not know how to imagine the oral period."[23] However, the problem has been and is being addressed—in two ways in particular.

One has stemmed from the fundamental research into folklore, particularly the research into the Homeric and Yugoslavian sagas, carried out by Milman Parry and Albert Lord.[24] This line of inquiry has generally been regarded as irrelevant to an understanding of the Gospel tradition. Folktales and sagas, often of considerable length and transmitted through generations of trained and dedicated poets and singers, cannot be expected to provide much of a guide to Jesus tradition of the Synoptic Gospels, where the teaching is characteristically aphoristic or in short stories (parables) and the period of transmission to be allowed for is no more than about fifty or sixty years or less. The study of oral tradition in different parts of Africa is largely

23. In E. P. Sanders and M. Davies, *Studying the Synoptic Gospels* (London: SCM, 1989), 141; ironically, in the same volume Sanders has demonstrated that there is an equal problem, too little recognized, of "imagining the literary period."

24. The work of A. B. Lord, *The Singer of Tales* (Cambridge, MA: Harvard University Press, 1978), has been seminal (here especially ch. 5).

subject to the same critique.[25] And anyway, it is becoming less relevant to our concerns since a paradigm shift took place in such folklore studies in the late 1970s and early 1980s, when a new emphasis on *performance* and the social interaction between performers and audiences directed attention away from the study of the *transmission* of oral tradition.[26]

The other line of research is more current—into the way *memory* works. Unfortunately, much of the research is flawed. Some scholars are content to think of memory only as it functions in regard to casual gossip of individuals and the serendipitous reminiscences of college reunions.[27] But this ignores the insight of the early form critics, that the oral tradition was *group* tradition; it existed in and for the churches; that is why it took the forms it did take. Likewise, the model of "oral history" drawn into the discussion recently by Samuel Byrskog,[28] while valuable in other aspects, also falls short at this point. *Oral history* envisages tradition as elicited from individual eyewitnesses by a historian some years or decades later, tradition that might have been latent or only casually exchanged in the meantime. But the *oral tradition* of the Gospels was self-evidently tradition used by the first churches and presumably at least in some degree formative of their beliefs and identity.

More to the point is the development of the theory of "social memory" and "cultural memory," associated with the names of Maurice Halbwachs[29] and Jan Assmann.[30] As the names indicate,

---

25. I refer particularly to J. Vansina, *Oral Tradition as History* (Madison: University of Wisconsin Press, 1985), a revision of his earlier *Oral Tradition: A Study in Historical Methodology* (London: Routledge & Kegan Paul, 1965); R. Finnegan, *Oral Literature in Africa* (Oxford: Clarendon, 1970); and I. Okpewho, *African Oral Literature: Backgrounds, Character and Continuity* (Bloomington: Indiana University Press, 1992).

26. I owe the observation to Annekie Joubert, who refers to R. Bauman and C. L. Briggs, "Poetics and Performance as Critical Perspectives on Language and Social Life," *Annual Review of Anthropology* 19 (1990): 59–88 (here 59–60).

27. E.g., Crossan seems to think of oral tradition principally in terms of individuals' casual recollection (*Birth of Christianity*, 49–93).

28. S. Byrskog, *Story as History—History as Story: The Gospel Tradition in the Context of Ancient Oral History*, WUNT 123 (Tübingen: Mohr Siebeck, 2000).

29. M. Halbwachs, *On Collective Memory* (ET: Chicago: University of Chicago Press, 1992).

30. J. Assmann, *Das kulturelle Gedächtnis: Schrift, Erinnerung und politische Identität in frühen Hochkulturen* (Munich: Beck, 1992).

here memory is seen to be conditioned or shaped by social or cultural factors. The main thrust of the theory is that memory selects and modifies the subject matter from the past in order to make it serviceable to the image that the community wishes to promote of itself. It is the *creative* rather than the *retentive* character of memory that social memory theory has brought to the fore. In this case my misgiving is at the failure to appreciate sufficiently the degree to which tradition can be both foundational and formative of group identity. And if, as I have argued, it was the impact of what Jesus said and did that first brought the disciple group together as disciples, it would follow that the tradition that gave them their identity as a group of disciples would be treasured by them, particularly during the period of Jesus' continuing mission, during which, as I argued in the first chapter, much of the tradition began to take its enduring shape.[31]

31. It is this emphasis on the impression made by the "impact" of Jesus' teaching and actions that marks the chief difference between my own understanding of the oral tradition process and that of Birger Gerhardsson, *Memory and Manuscript: Oral Tradition and Written Transmission in Rabbinic Judaism and Early Christianity* (Lund: Gleerup, 1961, 1998), for whom the term "memorization" plays the equivalent role. I can illustrate the difference between the two key terms (impact and memorization) most simply from my own experience. (1) I recall as a five- to eight-year-old memorizing my "times-tables"; it is only because it was so thoroughly drummed into me at that stage that I still know at once that eight sevens make fifty-six. But I also remember a mirror in the school cloakroom, on which was inscribed the motto, "You get back what you give, so smile." I didn't memorize that motto, but I recall it almost as readily as 8 x 7 = 56. The reason? It made such an impact on me, even as a five- to eight-year-old. It was so sensible, gave such a positive attitude to life, that it impressed itself on me in a lasting way. (2) I began to learn Greek at the age of twelve. I still value the hard slog of memorizing the paradigms of irregular verbs, since most of them come immediately to mind to this day as a result. But one of the first pieces of Greek I met was the classic epigram *Gnōthi s'auton*, "Know thyself." It made such an immediate impact on me that it became part of my personal philosophy from that day on. It was not a matter of having to memorize it. It simply left an indelible impression on my mind. (3) As a teenager and young man I memorized quite a lot of the NT. As a student in an exam on Bible knowledge, I remember being asked to outline Philippians. No problem, since I had memorized the text (King James Version). Much of that has faded now, not least since I have only rarely used the KJV since then. But my familiarity with the text of the Bible extends far beyond anything I memorized. I can recall the substance of many passages and quote some texts verbatim, not because I memorized them, but

In both cases, however, my main criticism is that these theories of memory have been framed, once again, in a literary culture. They do not take sufficient account of the differences that
might have been and almost certainly were involved in an oral
culture. In a culture that could not rely on widespread literacy
to disseminate wisdom or to propagate particular ideas, where
memory was much more trained to the retention of important
information, where skills had been developed in society and
among groups to ensure the preservation of memories important to these groups, the dynamic of memory was bound to be
different. That is why I did not attempt to develop such a theory
of memory in my *Jesus Remembered*, though I confess that the
title I chose has left me vulnerable to criticism on that score. The
more relevant line of inquiry, it seemed to me, was to explore how
oral traditions have been passed down in oral societies that we
can still access. In other words, the research into oral societies
and patterns of folklore appeared to be more relevant for our
understanding of the way the Jesus tradition was transmitted in
the oral period than present-day theories of memory.

In this enterprise I was much heartened by the little-known
work of Kenneth Bailey, who draws on some thirty years of experience in Middle Eastern villages.[32] These villages had retained
their identity over many generations, so that, arguably, their oral
culture is as close as we will ever be able to get to the village
culture of first-century Galilee. Characteristic of such culture,
Bailey points out, has been the gathering of the community at
the end of the day, when the sun has set and there are no other
distractions, to share the news of the day, to tell stories, to recall
matters of importance for the community. This gathering for
what is called *"haflat samar"* (social gathering for *samar*, which

---

because they made such an impact on me and because I have studied them
and reflected on them since, sometimes at great length. I imagine that the oral
Jesus tradition as we have it now is the result of a similar process. (4) In *Jesus
Remembered* (Grand Rapids: Eerdmans, 2003), I recall the impact made on me
by Kenneth Bailey's first recounting of two anecdotes from his own experience
(208n185). See further below (on Bailey) and the fourth point under the heading
"The Characteristic Features of Oral Tradition."

32. K. E. Bailey, "Informal Controlled Oral Tradition and the Synoptic Gospels," *Asia Journal of Theology* 5 (1991): 34–54; also "Middle Eastern Oral Tradition and the Synoptic Gospels," *ExpTim* 106 (1995): 363–67.

is cognate with the Hebrew *šāmar,* "to preserve") was how the community maintained its intellectual life and preserved its valued traditions. The peasants did this particularly by the rehearsal of traditional wisdom, the recitation of poems, and the retelling of stories, including not least stories from the village's own history.[33]

Of course, Bailey's work does not constitute scientific research; it is at best impressionistic and anecdotal. But it is precisely such experience that we are forced to rely on. Indeed, I suspect that it is precisely the difficulty in applying scientific methods to fast-disappearing oral cultures that has diverted so much recent research into performance and into the way memory functions in societies today. The question, however, is whether we can still gain some sense of the characteristic features of an oral traditioning procedure—a sense validated by such research into oral culture as has been possible, and also making sense of what we know of the earliest Christian community and of the shape that was early given to the Jesus tradition preserved in the Synoptic Gospels. I believe it is possible to speak sensibly of such characteristics.

The Characteristic Features of Oral Tradition

There are five characteristic features of the oral transmission of tradition that deserve attention.

First, and most obvious—or should be most obvious—an *oral performance* is *not* like reading a literary text.[34] In reading a text it is possible to look back a few pages to check what was written earlier. Having read the text, you can take it with you and read it again later. A written text can be revised, or edited, and so on. But none of that is possible with an oral tradition. An oral performance is evanescent. It is an *event.* It happens and then is gone. Oral tradition is not *there* for the auditor to check back a few pages, or to take away, or to edit and revise. It is not

33. Bailey, "Informal," 35–42; "Oral Tradition," 364–65; and earlier in his *Poet and Peasant: A Literary-Cultural Approach to the Parables in Luke* (Grand Rapids: Eerdmans, 1976), 31–32.
34. See, e.g., Finnegan, *Oral Literature,* 2–7.

a thing, an artifact like a literary text. That fact alone should be sufficient to cause us to question whether models of literary editing, intertextual dependence, or of archaeological layers are appropriate as we attempt to re-envisage the early transmission of the Jesus tradition.

How would this relate to the earliest Christian communities? The ones we know most about are, of course, the Pauline churches. Here the application is immediate—and somewhat surprising. It is surprising because we naturally think of communication between Paul and his churches in terms of letters—written documents. What we easily forget, however, is that communication of the letters within the churches would in most cases be by hearing and not reading. In that event they would not have been *read* by more than a few. For the great majority of recipients, the letter would have been *heard* rather than read. And the public reading of the text would require careful preparation and practice if it was to be heard meaningfully. The public reading of such a letter, in other words, would itself have the character of a performance.[35] This also means that general knowledge of and even reference back to such texts would depend much more on recollection of what had been heard when the text was read to the congregation than on an individual perusal of the text itself. In technical terms, oral tradition includes the phenomenon of *second orality*, that is, a written text known only through oral performance of the text. The same applies to the Gospels when they first became known to churches. They would have been read to the gathered congregations, and knowledge of them in most cases would be the knowledge of second orality, remembering what it was that had been read to them.

If this was the case for written communication to the first Christian churches, how much more for the earliest stage of the Jesus tradition when it was known only or at least predominantly in oral form. It would be partly a matter of transmission—the teaching of Jesus tradition to new churches; and partly a matter

35. The point is well made by W. Dabourne, *Purpose and Cause in Pauline Exegesis*, SNTSMS 104 (Cambridge: Cambridge University Press, 1999), ch. 8. See further P. J. Achtemeier, *"Omne verbum sonat*: The New Testament and the Oral Environment of Late Western Antiquity," *Journal of Biblical Literature* 109 (1990): 3–27.

of performance—recollection and celebration of, and instruction and reflection on, Jesus tradition already familiar to the disciple groups. And all this would happen in oral mode.

Second, as already indicated, oral tradition is essentially *communal* in character. On the literary paradigm we envisage an author writing for a reader. We speak of the intended reader, the ideal reader, the implied reader. We envisage the characteristic context of communication as the individual reader poring over the text, as the text there on a shelf to be consulted by readers functioning as individuals in separate one-to-one encounters with the text. But oral tradition continues in existence because there are communities for whom the tradition is important. The tradition is performed with greater or less regularity (depending on its importance) in the gatherings of the community, kept alive for the community by the elders, teachers, or those acknowledged as proficient performers of the tradition.

The recognition of this point has enabled J. M. Foley in recent years to merge oral-tradition theory fruitfully with receptionalist literary theory. For it is precisely the communal character of oral tradition, the degree to which the elders or teachers retain the tradition on behalf of the community and the performers perform it for the benefit of the community, that reminds us of the community's role in such performances. The performer's awareness that some tradition is already familiar to the community is a factor in the performance. The performance is heard within the community's "horizons of expectation." The performance's "gaps of indeterminacy" can be filled out from the audience's prior knowledge of the tradition or of like traditions. What Foley calls the "metonymic reference" of a performance enables the performer to use a whole sequence of allusions to the community's store of tradition and enables the community thus to recognize the consistency of the performance with the whole.[36]

When we apply this insight to the first churches, it again opens up new windows of potential understanding and insight. We can see at once why the letters of the NT, of James and Peter as well as of Paul, so little quote but appear often to allude to Jesus tradition. In churches already well versed in traditions of Jesus' teaching, repeated quotations and appeals to what Jesus said would

36. See below, 95n48.

have been unnecessary and ham-fisted. Much more effective in intracommunal and intercommunal communication would be allusions that sparked off particular and associated teachings within the communities' store of tradition and their communal knowledge of the Jesus tradition. It is no difficulty whatsoever to imagine the earliest disciple groups being reminded of something Jesus said or did and being similarly sparked to recall other similar teachings or events in Jesus' mission.[37]

Third, as already implied, in the oral community there would be one or more who were recognized as having *primary responsibility for maintaining and performing the community's tradition*—the singer of tales, the bard, the elders, the teachers, the rabbis. An ancient oral society had no libraries or dictionaries or encyclopedias. It instead had to rely on individuals whose role in their community was to function as, in the words of Jan Vansina, "a walking reference library."[38] In NT terms this certainly accords with the role of the apostle in providing what can properly be called foundation tradition for the churches he founded, as clearly attested in the Pauline letters.[39] And the prominence of teachers in the earliest communities, as widely attested across the spectrum of earliest Christian literature,[40] is best explained by the communities' reliance on them as repositories of community tradition.[41]

This in turn suggests that the teachers would be responsible for a body of teaching, presumably what Luke refers to as "the apostles' teaching" (Acts 2:42). There is no reason to conceive of this teaching as entirely fragmentary, a sequence of individual forms preserved randomly. In his paper on "The Gospels as Oral Traditional Literature," Albert Lord observes that "oral traditional composers think in terms of blocks and series of

37. See further Dunn, *Jesus Remembered*, 181–84.
38. Vansina, *Oral Tradition as History*, 37; similarly E. A. Havelock (*The Muse Learns to Write: Reflections on Orality and Literacy from Antiquity to the Present* [New Haven: Yale University Press, 1986]) speaks of an oral "encyclopedia" of social habit and custom-law and convention (57–58).
39. As in 1 Cor. 11:2, 23; 15:1–3; Phil. 4:9; Col. 2:6–7; 1 Thess. 4:1; 2 Thess. 2:15; 3:6.
40. Acts 13:1; Rom. 12:7; 1 Cor. 12:28–29; Gal. 6:6; Eph. 4:11; Heb. 5:12; James 3:1; Matt. 23:8; *Didache* 13.2; 15.1–2.
41. See further below, 96n52.

blocks of tradition."[42] The Synoptic tradition itself attests such groupings of parables (e.g., Mark 4:2–34) and miracle stories (4:35–5:43; 6:32–52), of Jesus' teaching on exorcism (3:23–29) or discipleship (8:34–37), of sequences of events such as a day in the life of Jesus (1:21–38), and so on. There is no justification for the common view that such groupings attest a later stage in the transmission of the Jesus tradition; on the contrary, the common view makes the unjustified assumption that oral tradition functioned only in fragments and single sayings. Our knowledge of how oral tradition "works" elsewhere, however, suggests that a grouping of like material would have been the pattern from earliest days, as soon as the stories and sayings of Jesus began to be valued by the groups of his followers.

Fourth, the more uncomfortable observation is that oral tradition subverts the idea(l) of an *"original"* version. With minds attuned to the literary paradigm, we envisage an original form, a first edition, from which all subsequent editions can at least in principle be traced by form and redaction criticism. We envisage tradition-history as an archaeological tell where we can in principle dig through the layers of literary strata to uncover the original layer, the "pure form" of Bultmann's conceptualization of *Formgeschichte*, form-history. But in oral tradition each performance is not related to its predecessors or successors in that way. In oral tradition, as Lord particularly has observed, *each* performance is, properly speaking, an *"original."*[43]

The point here can easily be misunderstood or misrepresented, so let me elaborate it a little. As it applies to the Jesus tradition, the point is *not* that there was no originating impulse that gave birth to the tradition. On the contrary, as I have argued in the first chapter, in at least many cases we can be wholly confident that there were things Jesus said and did that made an *impact* on his disciples, a *lasting* impact. But properly speaking, the *tradition* of the event is not the *event* itself. And the *tradition* of the saying is not the *saying* itself. The tradition is at best the *witness* of the event, and as there were presumably several witnesses, so

42. A. B. Lord, "The Gospels as Oral Traditional Literature," in *The Relationships among the Gospels*, ed. W. O. Walker (San Antonio: Trinity University Press, 1978), 33–91, here 59.
43. See below, 97n55.

there may well have been several traditions, or versions of the tradition, *from the first*. We can speak of an originating *event*; but we should certainly hesitate before speaking of an original *tradition* of the event. The same is true even of a saying of Jesus. The tradition of the saying attests the impact made by the saying on one or more of the original audience. But it may well have been heard slightly differently by others of that audience, and so told and retold in different versions *from the first*. And if, as Werner Kelber points out, Jesus himself used his most effective parables and aphorisms on more than one occasion, the ideal of a single original, authentic version once again reduces more to the figment of a literary-molded mind-set. Yes, we can and need to envisage teaching that originated with Jesus, actions that characterized his mission. But to treat the history of the Jesus tradition as though it were a matter of recovering some *original version of the tradition* is to conceptualize the transmission of the Jesus tradition at best misleadingly. This is one of the points on which the Jesus Seminar completely misjudged the character of the Jesus tradition.[44] In oral tradition, performance variation is integral to and even definitive of the tradition.[45]

Fifth and finally, oral tradition is characteristically (I do not say distinctively) a combination of *fixity* and *flexibility*, of *stability* and *diversity*. The preceding characteristics could easily be taken to encourage the idea of oral tradition as totally flexible and variable. That would be a mistake. In oral tradition there is characteristically a tale to be told, a teaching to be treasured, in and through and precisely by means of the varied performances. Oral tradition is oral memory; its primary function is to preserve and recall what is of importance from the past. Tradition, more or less by definition, embodies the concern for continuity with the past, a past drawn upon but also enlivened that it might illuminate the present and future. In the words of E. A. Havelock, "Variability and stability, conservatism and cre-

---

44. R. W. Funk and R. W. Hoover, eds., *The Five Gospels: The Search for the Authentic Words of Jesus* (New York: Macmillan, 1993); also R. W. Funk, *The Acts of Jesus: The Search for the Authentic Deeds of Jesus* (San Francisco: Harper/Polebridge, 1998).

45. A. Dundes, *Holy Writ as Oral Lit: The Bible as Folklore* (Lanham, MD: Rowman & Littlefield, 1999), 18–19, insists "upon 'multiple existence' and 'variation' as the two most salient characteristics of folklore."

ativity, evanescence and unpredictability all mark the pattern of oral transmission"—the "oral principle of 'variation within the same.'"[46] It is this combination, reverting to our second point, that makes it possible for the community both to acknowledge its tradition and to delight in the freshness of the individual performance. Moreover, the stability in a performed tradition is often to be found in the *theme* of the story or in its *core* element. On this point Robert Funk agrees: under the heading "Performance as gist; nucleus as core," he observes the "general rule in the study of folklore that oral storytellers reproduce the gist of stories in their oral performances. . . . As a consequence, historical reminiscence is likely to be found in the nucleus of stories, if anywhere."[47]

Here again it is not difficult to relate this to the Jesus tradition, even as we still find it in the Synoptic Gospels. For no one who is familiar with the Synoptic tradition could doubt that a characteristic of that tradition is precisely this feature of fixity and flexibility, of stability and diversity. As Funk observed in the same passage just quoted, the Synoptic evangelists "tend to reproduce the nucleus of a story—the core event—with greater fidelity than the introduction or conclusion." Indeed, it was this feature of the Synoptic tradition that initially sent me on the line of investigation that led to my *Jesus Remembered*. I wanted to understand better and if possible to explain why the Synoptic tradition takes the form that it does—where again and again and again we are confronted with what are obviously differing accounts of the same event, and differing versions of what in substance is clearly the same teaching. I have illustrated this feature elsewhere in sufficient detail and have no time to further illustrate it here.[48]

Of course, it is possible to explain such stability and diversity in terms of redaction criticism. But, as I have already pointed out, that always leaves the awkward gap of the "oral period" unfilled and unexplained. Now, however, it seems to me that in the understanding of how oral tradition "works" just sketched out,

---

46. Kelber, *Oral*, 33, 54; quoting E. A. Havelock, *Preface to Plato* (Cambridge, MA: Harvard University Press, 1963), 92, 147, 184, passim.

47. Funk, *Acts of Jesus*, 26.

48. See further Dunn, *Jesus Remembered*, ch. 8 and chs. 11–18; also "Altering the Default Setting," 160–69 [= 106–19 of the appendix].

we have the possibility of providing a fuller explanation for the process that resulted in the Synoptic tradition, an explanation that *includes* the oral period. Indeed, when we begin to shift out of the literary mind-set and to enter more into an oral mind-set, we may find we have an explanation for the Jesus tradition that is itself largely sufficient to explain that final character of the Synoptic tradition. We can see it as a tradition performed in many different ways before the literary effort of the Gospel writer who fixed his own performance more permanently in writing. It is this gap of "the oral period" that I hope my present work is beginning to fill in.

These five characteristic features of oral tradition, then, seem to fit and to fit remarkably well both what we know about the earliest churches and the Jesus tradition, and what we can guess to have been likely regarding both the teaching that bound these churches together and their communal life. This does not mean that all the features of the Gospel tradition can be wholly explained in terms of oral tradition. In particular, it is no part of my purpose to deny a literary connection between the Synoptic Gospels. Nor, of course, does my argument deny that the same features could be the result of literary composition and redaction. The Jesus tradition as we know it is, of course, in written form, and it remains natural to us, as ourselves people bred to the literary mind-set, to assume that an explanation in literary terms is always preferable. But the burden of my argument is that if we succumb to that natural inclination, we simply shut ourselves off from any understanding of what the Jesus tradition actually was and how it functioned in the oral period, in the twenty years or so following Jesus' mission. The brutal fact is that we simply cannot escape from a *presumption of orality* for the first stage of the transmission of the Jesus tradition. So if we are to "get back to Jesus of Nazareth" in any confident degree, we have no choice other than to use well-informed historical imagination to attempt to enter into what was happening to the Jesus tradition during that initial stage. I believe these identified characteristics of oral tradition help us to do just that.

At this point we can draw in the argument and conclusions from the first chapter. What we have done in the present chapter is, in effect, to work backward from the character of the Jesus

tradition as it still appears in the Jesus tradition. In contrast, in
the first chapter we attempted in effect to work forward from the
impact made by Jesus on his first disciples. One of the strengths
of my present thesis, it seems to me, is that the two approaches
seem to work together and to complement each other. By envisaging the oral period as indeed a gap to be crossed if we are
to get back to the context of Jesus' own mission, we can regard
the two approaches as the spans of a bridge pushing out from
either side of the gap. The theses of the two chapters, coming
at the problem from different sides of the gap, seem to meet in
the middle and thus to open up a viable way back to the first
witnesses of Jesus' mission.

What the two theses of these two chapters suggest is that those
who first became Jesus' disciples did so because of the impact
made on them by his ministry and teaching. This would include
not just those who literally followed him, but those whose lives
were heavily influenced by him, even though they did not leave
their homes—like Martha and Mary. Nor should we exclude
those in Galilean and other towns and villages whose lives became different as a result of an encounter with Jesus—people
such as Zacchaeus. What we have to imagine is that people like
that who had responded to Jesus and who had made some level
of commitment to him would inevitably have expressed that
commitment by meeting with others similarly impressed and
committed. They would share such impressions and memories,
partly, no doubt, to reassure themselves by checking whether
others felt about Jesus as they did. Similarly, when more formal
disciple groups emerged, the first "churches," we can readily and
appropriately imagine the members of such groups in a village
or a town gathering of an evening, when the sun had gone down
and there was nothing else to do, to hear again what had become
so important for them and to talk over the consequences for their
daily living. "Do you remember what he did/said when he . . . ?"
must have been a question often asked as the embryonic community began to feel and express its distinctiveness.[49]

49. Cf. Funk, *Acts of Jesus*, 2: "The followers of Jesus no doubt began to repeat
his witticisms and parables during his lifetime. They soon began to recount
stories about him."

It was presumably in such circumstances that the Jesus tradition began to be formulated. The unit of tradition began typically as a recollection by one or more disciples to their disciple group that was affirmed by the group and thus became part of their group tradition. It began as an expression of and testimony to the life-changing impact made by Jesus and recognized as such by the group. That is to say, the impact made by Jesus would not be something that was only put into traditional form days, months, or years later. The impact would *include* the formation of the tradition to recall what had made that impact. In making its mark the impacting word or event *became* the tradition of that word or event.[50] The stimulus of some word/story, the excitement (wonder, surprise) of some event would be expressed in the initial shared reaction;[51] the structure, the identifying elements, and the key words (core or climax) would be articulated in oral form as the group immediately recognized the significance of what had been said or happened. Thus established more or less immediately, these features would then be the constants, the stable themes that successive retellings could elaborate, and round which different performances could build their variations, as judged appropriate in the different circumstances. Subsequently, we may imagine a group of disciples meeting and requesting, for example, to hear again about the centurion of Capernaum, or about the widow and the treasury, or what it was that Jesus said about the tunic and the cloak, or about who is greater, or about the brother who sins. In response a senior disciple would again tell the appropriate story or teaching in whatever variant words and detail he/she judged appropriate for the occasion, with sufficient corporate memory ready to protest if one of the key elements was missed or varied too much.

In all this I have to insist again that such historical imagining does not take us back to Jesus himself (or to "the historical Jesus" as such). It envisages the earliest forms of the Jesus tradition as themselves evidence of the impact made by Jesus. It envis-

50. Cf. C. K. Barrett, *Jesus and the Gospel Tradition* (London: SPCK, 1967), 10, 16: "The tradition originated rather in the impression made by a charismatic person than in sayings learnt by rote. . . . It was preserved because it could not be forgotten."

51. Or should we be determined, come what may, to find a Jesus (reconstruct a "historical Jesus") who neither stimulated nor excited?

ages the reasons why the Jesus tradition takes the varied forms that we still find there. But it does not enable us, as it were, to encounter Jesus for himself, as though we could somehow step right through the Jesus tradition and come out the other side and meet him there. What it does is to enable the present-day disciple to sit with the earliest disciples and to share in their gatherings as they performed and celebrated their memories of Jesus, which were so important to them. To read and hear the teachings of Jesus and the stories of his mission is to join in a line of discipleship and continuity of church that stretches from the days of Jesus' own mission to the present.

But still the question will come: What does all this tell us about Jesus himself? If we can indeed share something of the impact he made as attested by the character of the Jesus tradition itself, can we speak more intelligibly about the one who made that impact? I think we can, but that is the subject of the next chapter.

3

THE CHARACTERISTIC JESUS

From Atomistic Exegesis
to Consistent Emphases

In these chapters I have been arguing that the quest of the historical Jesus has been largely unsuccessful because the earlier questers started from the wrong place, began with the wrong assumptions, and viewed the relevant data from the wrong perspective. In each case they forgot what should have been more obvious than it evidently has been and so lost the way almost from the beginning.

The first of these mistakes was to assume that faith was a hindrance to the quest, something that had to be stripped away if the quester was to gain a clear view of the historical Jesus. My response is that, on the contrary, the quest should start from the historical a priori that Jesus made a *faith impact* on his disciples, and that the only way to approach Jesus historically is to do so *through* that faith impact. In contrast to the older questers, the faith of the first disciples, not yet Easter faith, should not be stripped away, indeed cannot be stripped away, without throwing away the baby with the bathwater.

The second mistake has been to assume that the transmission of the Jesus tradition can be understood effectively only in *literary* terms, as a process of copying or editing earlier written sources. There has been a willing recognition on the part of most that the earliest Jesus tradition and earliest period of transmission of that tradition must have been *oral* in character. But there has been an almost complete failure to appreciate that such transmission could not have been like the literary process. There has been a consequent failure to take seriously the challenge to investigate how that tradition functioned in the oral period, and to ask whether the oral character of the earliest tradition could help us better understand the lasting and present form of the Jesus tradition. In contrast, it is my thesis that such an investigation can give us a clearer idea both of how the Jesus tradition first emerged and of its enduring character. That is, the character of the Synoptic Gospel tradition may have already been determined in large part during the oral period and before it was written down extensively in Mark and Q.

The third failure of previous quests has been the mistake of looking for a *distinctive* Jesus, distinctive in the sense of a Jesus *different* from his environment. This failure also has a twin aspect: first, the determination to find a non-Jewish Jesus; and second, the methodological assumption that the search should be directed toward identifying the particular saying or action that made Jesus stand out from his context most clearly.

Looking for the Non-Jewish Jesus

One of the most astonishing features of the quest of the historical Jesus has been the seeming determination of generation after generation of questers to discount or to strip away anything characteristically Jewish from the Jesus tradition. We can explain the underlying logic, even if we can never sympathize with it—the logic of traditional Christian anti-Semitism. As is well known, from the second century onward, perhaps we should say from the Epistle to the Hebrews onward, a consistent strand of Christian supersessionism has dominated Christian perception of the Jews.[1] This is the view that Christianity had superseded

1. Heb. 8:13; *Barnabas*; Melito, *Peri Pascha*; see further S. G. Wilson, *Related Strangers: Jews and Christians, 70–170 C.E.* (Minneapolis: Fortress, 1995).

Israel, had drained from its Jewish heritage all that was of value, and had left Judaism as an empty husk. On this view Christianity was antithetical to Judaism; indeed, the first time the word "Christianity" appears, in Ignatius of Antioch, early in the second century, it is coined as an antithesis to "Judaism."[2] Christianity, in other words, was early on perceived as not-Judaism, and Judaism as not-Christianity. The Jews, after all, had set themselves against the gospel and had rejected Christ; Judaism had thus set itself in opposition to Christianity. Worse still, the Jews had been responsible for Jesus' death. The people themselves had accepted this bloodguilt: "His blood be on us and on our children" (Matt. 27:25); they were deicides, murderers of God. What Jesus said of Judas was true of them all: "It would have been better for that man not to have been born" (Mark 14:21, author's translation). This was the underlying rationale behind the later persecutions and pogroms against the Jews in Christian Europe.

From this background emerged the governing instinct or assumption that Jesus himself cannot have been a Jew like that; he must have been different. And so we find as one of the most striking features of the quest repeated attempts to distance Jesus from his Jewish milieu. Susannah Heschel provides a penetrating analysis of this unsavory trend during the nineteenth century: "As Jewishness, Judaism represented a set of qualities associated with everything Christian theologians wished to reject and repudiate: false religiosity, immorality, legalism, hypocrisy, physicality, seductiveness, dishonesty, to name just a few."[3] She observes that liberal theologians painted "as negative a picture as possible of first-century Judaism" in order "to elevate Jesus as a unique religious figure who stood in sharp opposition to his Jewish surroundings."[4] A unique religious consciousness, unaffected by historical circumstances, in effect cut Jesus off from Judaism. Ernest Renan, for example, could write: "Funda-

2. Ign. *Magn.* 10.1–3; *Rom.* 3.3; *Phil.* 6.1; *Mart. Pol.* 10.1.
3. S. Heschel, *Abraham Geiger and the Jewish Jesus* (Chicago: University of Chicago Press, 1998), 75. On the anti-Jewishness of nineteenth-century NT scholarship, see particularly 66–75, 106–7, 117–18, 123, 153–57, 190–93, 212–13, 227. See also H. Moxnes, "Jesus the Jew: Dilemmas of Interpretation," in *Fair Play: Diversity and Conflicts in Early Christianity: Essays in Honour of Heikki Räisänen*, ed. I. Dunderberg et al. (Leiden: Brill, 2002), 83–103, here 83–89, 93–94.
4. Heschel, *Abraham Geiger*, 9, 21.

mentally there was nothing Jewish about Jesus"; after visiting
Jerusalem, Jesus "appears no more as a Jewish reformer, but
as a destroyer of Judaism. . . . Jesus was no longer a Jew."[5] And
for Albrecht Ritschl, the chief theological spokesman for liberal
Protestantism, Jesus' "renunciation of Judaism and its law . . .
became a sharp dividing line between his teachings and those
of the Jews."[6] Almost equally as striking is the fact that the great
account of the liberal quest by Albert Schweitzer simply failed
to take account of the substantial debate between Jewish and
Christian scholarship on the theme of Jesus the Jew.[7] On this
point the irony of liberalism is that it not only sought to "liberate" Jesus from the distorting layers of subsequent dogma, but
it also sought to present Jesus as the one who "liberated" the
quintessential spirit of religion from the "outmoded garb" of
Jewish cult and myth.

At the turn from the nineteenth to the twentieth century, Wil-
helm Bousset, in his little book on Jesus, well illustrates the twin
aspects of the liberal quest—the idealization of the Christian's
Jesus set starkly over against the vilification of his opponents
and of the religion they represented.

> The bitterest enemies of Jesus, and the true antipodes to all that
> he stood for, were the Scribes. However closely he resembled
> them in the outward forms of his activity, in the spirit of it he and
> they were at opposite poles. On the one hand was the artificiality
> of a hair-splitting and barren erudition, on the other the fresh
> directness of the layman and the son of the people; here was the
> product of long generations of misrepresentation and distortion,
> there was simplicity, plainness, and freedom; here a clinging to
> the petty and the insignificant, a burrowing in the dust, there a
> constant dwelling upon the essential and a great inward sense
> of reality; here the refinement of casuistry, formula- and phrase-
> mongering, there the straightforwardness, severity, and pitiless-
> ness of the preacher of repentance; here a language which was
> scarcely to be understood, there the inborn power of the mighty
> orator; here the letter of the law and there the living God. It was
> like the meeting of water and fire.[8]

5. Ibid., 156–57.
6. Ibid., 123.
7. Ibid., 3, 127.
8. W. Bousset, *Jesus* (ET: London: Williams & Norgate, 1906), 67–68.

Rudolf Bultmann's reaction to his liberal teachers included his own recognition that so far as NT theology was concerned, the proclamation of Jesus did indeed belong under the heading of "Judaism."[9] But his insistence was even stronger that faith had nothing to do with history, that therefore we need know nothing of this Jesus, and that the only thing that matters is an existential encounter with the kerygmatic Christ. Consequently, the outcome was not so very different: faith in the kerygmatic Christ was a quantum leap away from anything that might be shown to be true of the Jewish Jesus. And although the generation following Bultmann began to move away from his existentialism, they continued to regard the Judaism of Jesus' day with a jaundiced eye. Nothing shows this more clearly in German theology than the commonplace description of Second Temple Judaism as *Spätjudentum* (late Judaism)[10]—even though they well knew, of course, that Judaism continued to thrive and still flourishes to the present day. The logic again is clear, the assumption still that of Christian supersessionism: that Judaism's only function and purpose was to prepare for the coming of Christ and of Christianity; when Christ came, that marked the end of Judaism; the generation of Jesus' time was "late Judaism," the *last* Judaism. So too, with an astonishing insensitivity in the post-Holocaust period, it was not uncommon, even among prominent German theologians, to speak of Jesus doing away with Judaism or bringing Judaism to an end.[11]

In the renewed quest of the post-Bultmann era, most of the debate centered on the question of criteria, criteria that would enable the quester to determine whether any particular saying

9. R. Bultmann, *Theology of the New Testament*, vol. 1 (1948; ET: London: SCM; New York: Scribner, 1952), 3; similarly his *Primitive Christianity in Its Contemporary Setting* (ET: London: Thames & Hudson, 1956), 71–79.

10. See C. Klein, *Anti-Judaism in Christian Theology* (1975; ET: London: SPCK; Philadelphia: Fortress, 1978), here ch. 2; still in F. Hahn, *Christologische Hoheitstitel*, 5th ed. (Göttingen: Vandenhoeck, 1995), 133, 351; J. Becker, *Jesus of Nazareth* (Berlin: de Gruyter, 1998), e.g., 88, 224n146.

11. See, e.g., W. Pannenberg, *Jesus, God and Man* (ET: London: SCM, 1968), 255; L. Goppelt, *Theology of the New Testament*, vol. 1, *The Ministry of Jesus in Its Theological Significance* (1975; ET: Grand Rapids: Eerdmans, 1981), 97 ("Jesus actually superseded Judaism at its very roots through a new dimension"). See further J. T. Pawlikowski, *Christ in the Light of the Christian-Jewish Dialogue* (New York: Paulist, 1982), 37–47.

derived from Jesus himself. We will return to this subject in the
next section. Here we simply need to note that the principal
criterion, dissimilarity, tried to make a virtue out of what second
questers perceived as a necessity, by reconstructing their picture of Jesus out of what *distinguished* Jesus *from* his historical
context and set him over against his Jewish milieu. And the neo-
liberal quest of Dominic Crossan and Burton Mack differs from
the old liberal quest at this point only by its argument that the
influence of hellenization, which in Harnack's view marked out
the difference of the early church from Jesus, is already found
in Jesus' own teaching; despite the acknowledgment of Jesus'
Jewishness, the tendency is to play up the similarities between
Jesus' teaching with Hellenistic culture and the differences from
his native Jewish culture.[12] In other words, the Jewishness of
Jesus still remains an embarrassment to far too many attempt-
ing to take part in the quest.

In view of this embarrassment, it is a refreshing feature of the
other main strand of current inquiry into the life and teaching
of Jesus that it takes its start from the very point of embarrassment—Jesus the Jew. Indeed, my own preference is to limit
the title "the third quest of the historical Jesus" to the quest
for Jesus the Jew.[13] The prospects for such a (third) quest have
also been considerably improved by the fresh insights into the
character of Second Temple Judaism that have been granted to
scholarship during the past fifty years. Here the discovery of the
Dead Sea Scrolls has pride of place. More than anything else the
scrolls have broken open the idea of a monolithic, monochrome
Judaism, particularly as set over against the distinctiveness of
newly emerging Christianity. It has now become possible to
envisage Jesus, as also "the sect of the Nazarenes,"[14] within the
diversity of late Second Temple Judaism in a way that was hardly
thinkable before. This breakthrough has been accompanied and
reinforced by other important developments—particularly the

12. So, particularly, B. L. Mack, *A Myth of Innocence: Mark and Christian
Origins* (Philadelphia: Fortress, 1988), 73: "One seeks in vain (in original Jesus'
teaching), a direct engagement of specifically Jewish concerns"; the Jewish
apocalyptic prophet is replaced by the Hellenized Cynic teacher.
13. J. D. G. Dunn, *Jesus Remembered* (Grand Rapids: Eerdmans, 2003),
85–86 and n100.
14. Acts 24:5, 14; 28:22.

breakdown of the previously quite sharp distinction between
Judaism and Hellenism,[15] the recognition that the portrayals of
rabbinic Judaism in Mishnah and Talmud may not simply be
projected backward into the first century,[16] the renewed interest
in the rich range of apocryphal and pseudepigraphical Jewish
literature as further testimony to the diversity of Second Temple
Judaism,[17] and the increasing sophistication in evaluating the
steadily mounting archaeological data from the Israel (particularly Galilee) of Jesus' time.[18] In short, it is no exaggeration to
say that scholarship is in a stronger position than ever before to
sketch a clearer and sharper picture of Judaism in the land of
Israel at the time of Jesus and as the context of Jesus' ministry.
And, as Nils Dahl observed forty years ago: "Everything that
enlarges our knowledge of this environment of Jesus (Palestinian Judaism) indirectly extends our knowledge of the historical
Jesus himself."[19]

This third quest allows us to shift the goal of our search from
the *distinctive* and *different* Jesus to the *characteristic* Jesus. The
quest for a Jesus who is different from Judaism has led us down
some dubious roads and into some very unsavory places. To look
for a Jesus who was brought up in Galilee and carried through

15. M. Hengel, *Judaism and Hellenism*, 2 vols. (ET: London: SCM, 1974).

16. The many works of J. Neusner have been important here; see particularly
The Rabbinic Traditions about the Pharisees before 70, 3 vols. (Leiden: Brill, 1971);
also *From Politics to Piety: The Emergence of Rabbinic Judaism* (Englewood Cliffs,
NJ: Prentice Hall, 1973); and *Judaism: The Evidence of the Mishnah* (Chicago:
University of Chicago Press, 1981); see also on the one hand P. S. Alexander,
"Rabbinic Judaism and the New Testament," *Zeitschrift für die neutestament-
liche Wissenschaft* 74 (1983): 237–46; and on the other hand C. A. Evans, "Early
Rabbinic Sources and Jesus Research," in *Jesus in Context: Temple, Purity and
Restoration*, ed. B. Chilton and C. A. Evans (Leiden: Brill, 1997), 27–57.

17. See particularly J. H. Charlesworth, ed., *The Old Testament Pseudepigra-
pha*, 2 vols. (Garden City, NY: Doubleday; London: Darton, Longman & Todd,
1983–85); H. F. D. Sparks, ed., *The Apocryphal Old Testament* (Oxford: Clarendon, 1984).

18. See particularly J. H. Charlesworth, *Jesus within Judaism: New Light from
Exciting Archaeological Discoveries* (New York: Doubleday, 1988); also *Jesus and
Archaeology* (Grand Rapids: Eerdmans, forthcoming); J. L. Reed, *Archaeology
and the Galilean Jesus* (Harrisburg, PA: Trinity, 2000).

19. N. A. Dahl, "The Problem of the Historical Jesus" (1962), in *Jesus the
Christ: The Historical Origins of Christological Doctrine* (Minneapolis: Fortress,
1991), 81–111, here 96.

most of his mission there, and yet who distanced himself fundamentally from the practice and beliefs of his fellow Galilean Jews, was always bound to end up with a rather odd Jesus. But a Jesus who was brought up in Galilee and who could evidently empathize with typical Galilean Jews suggests rather that the Jewishness of Jesus is a valid and viable starting point for the quest, rather than something to be stripped away or shied away from. We should, of course, not go to the opposite extreme of assuming that Jesus would be characteristically Jewish through and through. Those who have pioneered this new way of looking at Jesus, particularly Geza Vermes and Ed Sanders, are open to criticism at this precise point—that they have minimized the tensions between Jesus and the Pharisees in particular.[20] Jesus appears to be such a good Jew that his denunciation by the high priestly party and execution become something of a puzzle. In closing the gap between Jesus and Judaism, such scholars open up the other gap, the one between Jesus and the Christianity which followed.[21]

Nevertheless, looking at Jesus within the context of the Judaism of his time remains a more plausible line of search than starting with the intent of wrenching him out from that context. By noting what the characteristics are of Jewish practice and belief, we can infer, unless we have indications to the contrary, that Jesus shared these characteristics. A basic list would include the fact that he was circumcised, that he was brought up to say the Shema, to respect the Torah, to attend the synagogue, to observe the Sabbath. In addition, Sanders has offered a list of what he describes as "almost indisputable facts" about Jesus:

20. G. Vermes, *Jesus the Jew* (London: Collins, 1973); also *The Religion of Jesus the Jew* (London: SCM, 1993); E. P. Sanders, *Jesus and Judaism* (London: SCM, 1985); also *The Historical Figure of Jesus* (London: Penguin, 1993).

21. Cf. D. A. Hagner, *The Jewish Reclamation of Jesus: An Analysis and Critique of the Modern Jewish Study of Jesus* (Grand Rapids: Zondervan, 1984), who argues that "the Jewish reclamation of Jesus has been possible only by being unfair to the Gospels" (14); "it is always Jesus the Jew they are interested in and not the Jesus of Christianity" (38). Even N. T. Wright's reappraisal of Jesus' mission (*Jesus and the Victory of God*), while thoroughly "third quest" in character, leaves something of an awkward gap between the climax that he portrays Jesus as expecting and the outcome that follows, which his further volume in the series (*The Resurrection of the Son of God* [London: SPCK, 2003]) fails adequately to bridge.

that his mission mainly operated round the towns and villages of Galilee; that the main emphasis of his preaching was the kingdom of God; that he characteristically taught in aphorisms and parables; and so on.[22] Here again, what emerges is a picture of the characteristic Jesus.

This is a theme I will want to develop in the final section of this chapter, but at this point let me move on to my second main critique of the earlier quest.

Turning Pyramids Upside Down

If the first mistake of the earlier quests has been to search for a non-Jewish Jesus, the second mistake has been to make success dependent on identifying some key saying or action whose historicity can be demonstrated with high probability, and which then becomes the base round which other material coheres and on which a reconstruction of the historical Jesus' mission can be attempted.

This has become a feature of the quest as it was renewed by Bultmann's pupils. It can be summed up as the quest for *criteria*, criteria in particular by means of which any specific saying of Jesus can be recognized to have derived from Jesus. The assumption is still the one criticized in the previous chapters, that the only option for the quester is to attempt to burrow through the layers of tradition that intervene between Jesus' mission and the Synoptic tradition. The assumption is still that these layers reflect primarily the subsequent faith of the early churches, that between each layer there is, as it were, an often-impenetrable mortar of post-Easter faith. The assumption is still that the original layer consisted only of isolated units and individual forms. The only hope, then, is to find places where the mortar is thin or weak and where a determined effort can succeed in pushing through it, eventually to arrive at the earliest form of some individual saying, which can then be attributed to Jesus.

There have been many attempts to identify the criteria that give most hope of attaining this goal. The most famous was the one already referred to, the criterion or criteria of *dissimilarity*.

22. Sanders, *Jesus*, 11, 17, 321, 326; also *Historical Figure*, 10–11.

Norman Perrin defined this criterion most clearly: "The earliest form of a saying we can reach may be regarded as authentic if it can be shown to be dissimilar to characteristic emphases both of ancient Judaism and of the early Church."[23] The point was not that only sayings that satisfied this criterion should be recognized as authentic, but rather that such sayings will be the only ones we can *know* to be genuine.[24] Perrin backed up this first criterion with a second, "the criterion of coherence": "material from the earliest strata of the tradition may be accepted as authentic if it can be shown to cohere with material established as authentic by means of the criterion of dissimilarity."[25] And with some hesitation he added a third, "the criterion of multiple attestation": "authentic material which is attested in all, or most, of the sources which can be discerned behind the synoptic gospels."[26]

As the discussion of criteria broadened out beyond the confines of the new quest properly so called, other criteria have been offered, not necessarily as alternatives, but in addition. For example, Joachim Jeremias in effect offered the criterion of characteristic style traceable back to Aramaic forms;[27] John P. Meier has given some prominence to "the criterion of embarrassment";[28] and Gerd Theissen (with Dagmar Winter) presses the criterion of historical plausibility.[29] But the criterion of dissimilarity still impresses many questers because it offers the most credible results: if a unit of tradition shows no influence from the Judaism of the time and no influence of post-Easter faith, then it can be attributed to Jesus himself with confidence as the most plausible explanation for its presence in the Jesus tradition.

23. N. Perrin, *Rediscovering the Teaching of Jesus* (London: SCM, 1967), 39.
24. R. S. Barbour, *Traditio-Historical Criticism of the Gospels* (London: SPCK, 1972).
25. Perrin, *Rediscovering*, 43.
26. Ibid., 45.
27. J. Jeremias, *New Testament Theology*, vol. 1, *The Proclamation of Jesus* (ET: London: SCM, 1971), part 1. See also M. Casey, *Aramaic Sources of Mark's Gospel*, SNTSMS 102 (Cambridge: Cambridge University Press, 1998); also *An Aramaic Approach to Q*, SNTSMS 122 (Cambridge: Cambridge University Press, 2002).
28. J. P. Meier, *The Marginal Jew: Rethinking the Historical Jesus*, vol. 1 (New York: Doubleday, 1991), 168–71.
29. G. Theissen and D. Winter, *The Quest for the Plausible Jesus: The Question of Criteria* (ET: Louisville: Westminster John Knox, 2002), 172–225.

It is not so much that I object to the logic of this. What I object to here, rather, is that it makes so much of what can be said about Jesus to depend on a single saying or small group of sayings. Likewise, the criterion of embarrassment gives premium value to any oddball saying within the Jesus tradition. And although Sanders is very conscious of the dangers, he then proceeds to make much of his own reconstruction dependent on his own entry point into the Jesus tradition, that is, his interpretation of the "cleansing of the Temple."[30] In all this there is a danger of inverting the pyramid: of trying to build up a portrayal and understanding of Jesus on the basis of sometimes a single verse, a narrow base and a top-heavy conclusion, the former probably too small to sustain the latter. No wonder so many pictures of the historical Jesus come crashing down after a time!

So, for example, Ernst Käsemann began the second quest for the historical Jesus by identifying "the distinctive element in the mission of Jesus" as the authority claimed by Jesus for his teaching over against Moses, as attested in the antitheses of Matt. 5.[31] Günther Bornkamm found the distinguishing feature in the note of eschatological fulfillment in Jesus' proclamation.[32] On the basis of Mark 9:1, Werner Kümmel felt able to conclude that a distinctive feature of Jesus' teaching was his expectation that the coming of the kingdom was imminent.[33] Heinz Schürmann found that the Lord's Prayer for the kingdom to come (Matt. 6:10//Luke 11:2) is the surest way into Jesus' understanding of the kingdom.[34] More typical has been the confidence that Matt. 12:28//Luke 11:20 provides a sure entry into Jesus' understanding of the kingdom as already present.[35] The disputes as to which of the Son of Man sayings in the Gospels are "original" and "au-

30. Sanders, Jesus, 4–5, and ch. 1: "Jesus and the Temple" (61–76).

31. E. Käsemann, "The Problem of the Historical Jesus," in Essays on New Testament Themes (ET: London: SCM, 1964), 15–47, here 37–45.

32. G. Bornkamm, Jesus of Nazareth (1956; ET: London: Hodder & Stoughton, 1960), 67.

33. W. G. Kümmel, "Eschatological Expectation in the Proclamation of Jesus," in The Future of Our Religious Past: Essays in Honour of Rudolf Bultmann, ed. J. M. Robinson (ET: London: SCM, 1971), 29–48, here 39–41.

34. H. Schürmann, Gottes Reich—Jesu Geschick: Jesu ureigener Tod im Licht seiner Basileia-Verkündigung (Freiburg: Herder, 1983), 135, 144.

35. E.g., W. D. Davies and D. C. Allison, Matthew, vol. 2 (Edinburgh: Clark, 1991): "one of the assured results of modern criticism" (239).

thentic" are legion.[36] As already noted, the Jesus Seminar finds the hallmark feature of Jesus' teaching in his aphoristic sayings. Examples could be multiplied.

In each case, however, it would be possible to collect a longer list of those who question each of the claims. For every scholar who builds his inverted pyramid on this saying or that, this passage or that, there are many more scholars who are trying to push the pyramid off its all-too-narrow base. In other words, there is an obvious danger in making one's objective the identification of a sure original and authentic item of the Jesus tradition, with a view to building round it as the outer walls of a castle would in olden days be built round the inner keep. The danger is that the inner keep is itself liable to be undermined by the maze of other tunnels dug through the mass of the Jesus tradition, or that onslaughts on the keep itself ensure that the outer walls are never very effective. Or, to change the metaphor again, the danger is that the enterprise will be caught in the swamp of endless dispute about the value of this saying or that, a swamp into which many questers wander only to find themselves bogged down in multiplying hypotheses and unable to move forward with any confidence. As Sanders put it: the view "that a sufficiently careful exegesis of the sayings material will lead to 'a correct decision,' has led many a New Testament scholar into a quagmire from which he has never emerged."[37] Or, to vary the metaphor yet again, in adaptation of Albert Schweitzer's famous image,[38] the complexity of the Jesus tradition timetable means that the questers often find themselves stopped at intermediate stations with a forward connection no longer guaranteed and little hope that a through train will follow in due course.

In the face of such despondency my suggestion is that we should take the wise comment of Leander Keck as pointing the way forward: "Instead of the *distinctive* Jesus we ought rather to seek the *characteristic* Jesus."[39] Let us give up the quest for that which distinguished Jesus from his context and seek instead the

---

36. See, e.g., the brief review of options in Dunn, *Jesus Remembered*, 734–36.
37. Sanders, *Jesus*, 131.
38. A. Schweitzer, *The Quest of the Historical Jesus* (1906; London: SCM, 2000), 299.
39. L. E. Keck, *A Future for the Historical Jesus* (Nashville: Abingdon, 1971), 33 (my emphasis).

characteristic Jesus, both that which was characteristic of Jesus as a Jew and that which is characteristic of the Jesus tradition as it now stands.

The Characteristic Jesus

If the theses being argued in these chapters are correct, then what we are looking at in the Jesus tradition, and what we are looking for through the Jesus tradition, is one whose mission was remembered for a number of features, each illustrated by stories and teaching, performed in the disciple circles and church gatherings, though not yet (properly speaking) "documented" (the literary paradigm). H. Strasburger has put the claim more boldly than I would:

> The very abundance of historical inconsistencies speaks in favour of an . . . untidy, but certainly developed oral tradition whose honest basic effort at the beginnings of the formation of tradition was apparently to preserve as precise as possible a memory of Jesus, his teaching and proclamation, that is, to give a true and historical witness. And precisely this unique, unfalsifiable *overall impression* has undoubtedly been preserved in the canonical gospels . . . no matter how many details in the accounts may still, and perhaps forever, remain disputable.[40]

If that is overbold, a concern nevertheless to identify the "overall impression" rather than the specific detail, the characteristic rather than the different Jesus, indicates a viable broad-brush criterion for the would-be quester, to which appeal should be made before turning to particular detail. The criterion is this: any feature that is *characteristic within the Jesus tradition, even if only relatively distinctive of the Jesus tradition*, is most likely to go back to Jesus,[41] that is, to reflect the original impact made

---

40. H. Strasburger, "Die Bibel in der Sicht eines Althistorikers," in *Studien zur alten Geschichte* (Hildesheim: Olms, 1990), 317–39, here 336–37, cited by M. Reiser, "Eschatology in the Proclamation of Jesus," in *Jesus, Mark and Q: The Teaching of Jesus and Its Earliest Records*, ed. M. Labahn and A. Schmidt (Sheffield: Sheffield Academic Press, 2001), 216–38, here 223 (my italics).

41. As R. W. Funk notes, "distinctive" is a better historical category than "dissimilar" (*Honest to Jesus* [San Francisco: HarperSanFrancisco, 1996], 145).

by Jesus' teaching and actions on several at least of his first disciples. The logic is straightforward: if a feature is character- istic within and relatively distinctive of the Jesus tradition (in comparison with other Jewish traditions), then the most obvi- ous explanation of its presence in the Jesus tradition is that it reflects the abiding impression that Jesus made on at least many of his first followers, an impact that first drew them into and constituted their community with other disciples, and which was celebrated (together with the kerygmatic traditions of cross and resurrection) in the gatherings of the first churches through the first generation of Christianity.

This will not mean, of course, that every item in a characteris- tic motif can be traced back to something heard or witnessed by Jesus' first disciples. The more characteristic a motif, the more likely it is to have been elaborated and extended. But equally, the more characteristic a motif is, the *less* likely it is to have been first inserted into the Jesus tradition some years after the tradi- tion had begun to circulate and be celebrated in oral mode. The more characteristic a feature is across the various strands of the Jesus tradition, the more likely it is that the feature reflects the impact Jesus made on his disciples rather than the inspiration of some unknown disciple operating in Galilee or Jerusalem or Antioch. The point is that such an impression of Jesus gained by observing such characteristic features of the Jesus tradi- tion is not dependent on any one or any particular saying. It is precisely the impression made by the motif that indicates the overall impression made by Jesus, that this was the sort of thing he said and did, that he spoke and acted in this way frequently or regularly.

It is not difficult to illustrate the effectiveness of this way of proceeding in the quest; most of the illustrations that fol- low are ones that I have elaborated at some length in *Jesus Remembered*.

Consider again the Jewishness of Jesus. Within the Jesus tradition there is a consistent interest in typically Jewish con- cerns—what obedience to the Torah involves, how to observe the Sabbath, what counts as clean and unclean, attendance at syna- gogue, the purity of the temple.[42] It can scarcely be doubted that

42. E.g., Matt. 5:17–48; Mark 2:23–3:5; 7:1–23; Luke 4:16; 19:45–48.

Jesus shared such concerns. What his attitude was on particular issues is open to debate and evidently was a matter of some debate among those responsible for rehearsing and passing on the Jesus tradition;[43] but that he himself was engaged with such issues during his mission is clear beyond reasonable doubt. In the same connection, Jesus is consistently shown as engaged in dialogue and dispute with Pharisees. Here we can see how the tradition has been elaborated, with Matthew in particular extending the motif of debate with Pharisees quite substantially.[44] But that is obviously the way to express the point: Matthew *extended* a motif *already thoroughly integrated* within the Jesus tradition; Jesus was well remembered for his spats with various Pharisees. Despite the anti-Jewishness of previous phases of the quest, the Jewishness of Jesus' concerns is not in question.

Or again, it can hardly be doubted that Jesus spent much if not most of his mission in Galilee. The Synoptic tradition is so consistent on the point and the Galilean provenance of the Synoptic accounts so clear that it would be ludicrous to argue otherwise. It is not simply the fact that Jesus' mission is clearly remembered as being carried out predominantly round the Sea of Galilee and its nearby villages. But Jesus' parables in particular are shot through with agricultural references and echoes of what we know to have been the social situation in Galilee—wealthy estate owners, resentment over absentee landlords, exploitative stewards of estates, family feuds over inheritance, debt, day laborers, and so on.[45] To be sure, the Johannine account indicates a much more Jerusalem-centered mission, though even so three of the first four of John's "signs" are located in Galilee. The resulting tensions between the Synoptics and John are unlikely

43. We need only compare the different ways in which Mark and Matthew portray Jesus' attitude to the law, as exemplified by the contrast between Mark 7:15, 19 and Matt. 15:11; see further Dunn, *Jesus Remembered*, 563–83.

44. Details in my "The Question of Anti-Semitism in the New Testament Writings of the Period," in *Jews and Christians: The Parting of the Ways, A.D. 70 to 135; The Second Durham-Tübingen Research Symposium on Earliest Christianity and Judaism, Durham, September 1989*, ed. J. D. G. Dunn (Tübingen: Mohr Siebeck, 1992), 177–211, here 205.

45. See, e.g., S. Freyne, "Jesus and the Urban Culture of Galilee," in *Galilee and Gospel*, WUNT 125 (Tübingen: Mohr Siebeck, 2000), 183–207, here 195–96, 205–6; and further S. Freyne, *Galilee, Jesus and the Gospels* (Dublin: Gill & Macmillan, 1988).

ever to be satisfactorily resolved, but that does not change the
overall impression that Jesus was a Galilean Jew whose mission
was largely shaped by and focused on the circumstances of his
Galilean homeland.

A third example is obviously Jesus' preaching of the kingdom
or royal rule of God. Here again, no one who takes the Synoptic
tradition seriously could even begin to doubt that the kingdom
of God was at the center of Jesus' mission. That is, the royal rule
of God was certainly a characteristic theme of his message, and
as it happens was also fairly distinctive of Jesus' preaching in
comparison both with the Judaism of his own time and with the
Christianity that followed.[46] At this point, too, the comparative
scarcity of references to the kingdom in John's version of Jesus'
mission remains something of a problem for the historian of the
Jesus tradition,[47] but that fact hardly diminishes the overwhelming impression given by the Synoptic Gospels. Proclamation of
God's royal rule was one of the most characteristic features of
Jesus' mission. Consequently, it hardly matters that we cannot
be sure whether, for example, Mark 1:15—"The time is fulfilled,
and the kingdom of God has come near; repent, and believe in
the good news"—records accurately what Jesus actually said on
entering Galilee or is Mark's own summary of Jesus' preaching.
The point is that the motif is so well rooted in the Jesus tradition that a Markan summary is almost equally as effective in
communicating the overall impression made by Jesus' kingdom
preaching.

Of course, students of the Gospels know that there are two
strands in the Synoptic kingdom motif: the kingdom as future
though imminent, and the kingdom as already present and active through Jesus' ministry. They are also well aware that there
has been a huge and long-lasting debate as to which of these
two strands is the more "original." This debate demonstrates
more clearly than most others the futility of making conclusions
regarding "the historical Jesus" depend on individual verses and
what can be inferred from them. The fact is that *both* strands
are well rooted in and run through the Synoptic tradition.[48] Both

46. For details, see Dunn, *Jesus Remembered,* 383–87.
47. Details in ibid., 384n8.
48. Full documentation can be found in ibid., ch. 12.

are characteristic of the Synoptic Jesus. How dare we exegetes and expositors insist on squeezing such diverse traditions into a *single* mold and on squeezing *out* what does not fit our own ideas of consistency and good sense? It is much more responsible for historians and exegetes to recognize that this double characteristic of the Jesus tradition is best explained as a double characteristic of Jesus' own teaching and mission. The overall two-sided impact of Jesus remains clear, even if it remains unclear how the two sides were held together by Jesus and his first disciples.

A fourth obvious example is the son of man/Son of Man tradition in the Gospels.[49] Here again, the picture is clear beyond peradventure. The tradition that Jesus used the phrase "son of man" is so thoroughly rooted in the Gospel tradition, and so conspicuous by its relative disuse in the Judaism of Jesus' day, as by its almost total absence from early Christian tradition elsewhere,[50] that on any sensible reckoning it can have originated only within the Jesus tradition. What is also striking is that the phrase appears so consistently on Jesus' own lips. It is not an identifying label used by others: Is Jesus the Son of Man? It is not a confession used by his disciples: Jesus is the Son of Man. All that the tradition requires us to say—but it does require us to say it—is that Jesus himself used the phrase. Here again, this compelling deduction does not require us to argue that every son of man/Son of Man saying derived directly from Jesus. But the fact that any working over of the tradition worked within the tradition of a phrase used only by Jesus assuredly confirms that *the original form of the tradition derived directly from and directly reflects Jesus' own characteristic usage.* On the basis of the data it is also possible to argue that the titular usage "the Son of Man" is in some/many cases at least a firming up of the Aramaic idiom, "the son of man," that is, "someone," "a man like me." What is not credible as an explanation for the data is that the complete motif was initially inserted into the Jesus tradition at a post-Easter or

49. For what follows see the detailed discussion in ibid., 724–61, 798–802, 806–7.
50. It appears as a title elsewhere in the NT only in Acts 7:56. In Heb. 2:6; Rev. 1:13; and 14:14, it is not a title but a reference to the OT passages Ps. 8:4 and Dan. 7:13.

later stage. That some scholars should continue to argue to that effect,[51] despite the overwhelming testimony of the data, is in my view an example of methodological perversity.

It is with regard to the son of man/Son of Man sayings that the tendency to set individual verses in antithesis to each other, and to use one to disqualify the other as evidence of Jesus' own usage, has run amok. If Jesus spoke of the son of man in terms of his present activity, he evidently cannot also have spoken of the suffering Son of Man or of the coming Son of Man! If Jesus looked for vindication in or through the Son of Man, he cannot have used the phrase to describe his own mission![52] Here again, a twentieth-century logic has been imported into the debate, and atomistic exegesis has been used to fragment a complex but quite plausibly coherent motif. To be sure, there is scope for debating how a philological idiom ("son of man" = "man," "one") could cohere with reference to the vision of Dan. 7 ("one like a son of man" [RSV] coming on clouds to the Ancient of Days). The point here, however, is that both usages are well rooted in and quite well spread across the Jesus tradition. A search for the characteristic rather than the idiosyncratic Jesus suggests that we should try to make sense of *both* emphases within the son of man/Son of Man material before assigning one or the other to subsequent christological redaction.

The kingdom of God and the son of man/Son of Man traditions in the Synoptic Gospels provide the best examples of the case for and value of a search for the characteristic Jesus rather than the differently distinctive Jesus. The examples could easily be multiplied. It is clear, for instance, that Jesus was known as a highly successful exorcist: his success as an exorcist and his reputation as an exorcist are both clearly attested in the Jesus tradition; and more than one collection of Jesus' teaching on the subject has been preserved within the Synoptic tradition.[53] Whatever might be made of particular instances of exorcism in Jesus' mission, it can hardly be denied that he acted as an exorcist and healed people who were possessed. It would be odd indeed if a scholar accepted that Jesus acted as an exorcist but refused

51. Bibliography in Dunn, *Jesus Remembered*, 736nn128, 131.
52. Bibliography again in ibid., 734–36.
53. Ibid., 670–77.

to accept that any of the actual accounts of Jesus' exorcisms are based on sound memories of events in Jesus' mission. It is equally self-evident, but in this case much less controversial, that Jesus was an effective teacher of aphoristic and parabolic wisdom. The characteristic Jesus was a parabolist, a *mošēl*, one who typically spoke in parables and pithy sayings (*mĕšālîm*).

More striking for its characteristic distinctiveness is Jesus' use of the term "Amen." The term is familiar in both Hebrew and Aramaic (*ʾāmēn*) and marks a strong solemn affirmation of what has been said, most typically in a formal liturgical context. And the Jesus tradition gives clear testimony that Jesus used the term consistently in his own teaching.[54] But he did so in a quite distinctive way. For whereas in regular usage "Amen" affirmed or endorsed the words of someone else, in the Jesus tradition the term is used without exception to introduce and endorse Jesus' *own* words.[55] This quite unique usage can hardly be attributed to the early Christians; their own use of "Amen" was in accord with the traditional pattern.[56] Of course, once again, we can hardly exclude the likelihood that in performing the tradition the tradents/teachers extended the motif within the tradition. But neither can it be seriously doubted that the usage began with Jesus and was a characteristically distinctive feature of his own teaching style. Why else would the term have been retained throughout the Jesus tradition and in transliterated form? That must be one of the most secure conclusions capable of being derived from a serious engagement with the tradition-history of Jesus' teaching. And an obvious corollary lies close to hand: that Jesus used this formula to call attention to what he was about to say and to give it added weight.

Finally, two other characteristic features of the Jesus tradition are worth noting, one because it is surprisingly neglected, and the other because it runs counter to a thesis at present widely influential. The first is the fact that the Jesus tradition is consistently

54. Details in ibid., 700–701.

55. J. Jeremias, *The Prayers of Jesus* (ET: London: SCM, 1967), 112–15: "It has been pointed out almost ad nauseam that a new use of the word *amen* emerged in the four gospels which is *without analogy in the whole of Jewish literature and in the rest of the New Testament*" (112).

56. Of some thirty other examples in the NT, 1 Cor. 14:16 is the most interesting; otherwise it is characteristically attached to the end of a doxology.

presented as having a starting point in the mission of John the Baptist. This is attested not only in each of the four Gospels, but the collection of teaching material known as Q also begins with John the Baptist tradition, as do the summary presentations of the good news regarding Jesus in Acts (1:21–22; 10:37). What this suggests is that the Jesus tradition was always seen as having a narrative shape, as recalling a mission with a particular starting point. This in turn suggests that the Gospel shape of the Jesus story actually reflects the shape both of Jesus' actual mission and of the earliest disciples' rememberings of it.

Second, the motif of judgment on "this generation" is widely regarded as reflecting negative experiences in the later Christian mission and consequently as indicating redaction of the Q document.[57] But here again, the motif is widespread in the Synoptic tradition and relatively absent elsewhere, which surely indicates, yet once again, that this was a characteristic motif of Jesus' own preaching and that it was recalled and retained within the Jesus tradition for the same reason.[58] What kind of idealization of "the historical Jesus" prevents us from concluding that Jesus also expressed some irritation at the negative response to his message?

To sum up, it is not difficult to build up a picture of the characteristic Jesus—a Jesus who began his mission from his encounter with John the Baptist; a Jew who operated within Galilee, within the framework of the Judaism of the period and in debate with others influential in shaping the Judaism of the period; a Jesus who characteristically proclaimed the royal rule of God both as coming to full effect soon and as already active through his ministry; a Jesus who regularly used the phrase "the son of man," probably as a way of speaking of his own mission and of his expectations regarding its outcome; a Jesus who was a successful exorcist and knew it; a Jesus whose characteristic mode of teaching was in aphorisms and parables; a Jesus whose "Amen" idiom expressed a high evaluation of the importance of what he said; a Jesus who reacted strongly against the apathy and disdain that his message frequently encountered.

57. See those cited in Dunn, *Jesus Remembered*, 421n207.
58. Ibid., 468n397.

I could go on to amass further characteristics of the characteristic Jesus, but hopefully enough has already been said to indicate how substantial a portrayal can readily be achieved by simply directing our quest to the characteristic Jesus. I repeat, such a reconstruction does not guarantee the historical accuracy of recall of any particular saying or episode. But the method must certainly provide a much sounder basis for a historical reconstruction than one that depends on the evaluation of particular sayings and episodes. Not only so, but a recognition that a motif is firmly rooted within and across the Jesus tradition may be the decisive factor in deciding the witness-value of particular sayings and episodes. The presence of such a characteristic motif, in fact, begins to reverse the normal twentieth-century burden-of-proof argument. Where a particular saying or episode reflects such a characteristic motif, scholarship should be asking not "Why should it be attributed to Jesus?" but "Why should it *not* be attributed to Jesus?"

From these three chapters I therefore conclude: *Remembering Jesus* really means what it says, that the Jesus tradition was a way of remembering Jesus, showing how Jesus was remembered, and enabling us today still to share in these rememberings. My threefold thesis can be summed up simply. First, Jesus made an impact on those who became his first disciples, well before his death and resurrection. That impact was expressed in the first formulations of the Jesus tradition, formulations already stable before the influence of his death and resurrection was experienced. Second, the mode of oral performance and oral transmission of these formulations means that the force of that original impact continued to be expressed through them, notwithstanding or rather precisely because the performances were varied to suit different audiences and situations. As its lasting form still attests, the Jesus tradition was neither fixed nor static, but living in quality and effect. And third, the characteristic features running through and across the Jesus tradition give us a clear indication of the impression Jesus made on his disciples during his mission. As that doyen of British NT scholarship, C. H. Dodd, put it in his last significant book: "The first three gospels offer a body of sayings on the whole so consistent, so coherent, and withal so distinctive in manner, style and content, that no reasonable critic should doubt, whatever reservations he may have about individual sayings, that we find here reflected the thought of a single, unique teacher."[59] The resulting picture of Jesus is not an objective description. There is no credible "historical Jesus" behind the Gospel portrayal different from the characteristic Jesus of the Synoptic tradition. There is no Galilean Jesus available to us other than the one who left such a strong impression in and through the Jesus tradition. But this assuredly is the historical Jesus that the Christian wants to encounter. And should the scholar and historian be content with anything less?

59. C. H. Dodd, *The Founder of Christianity* (London: Collins, 1971), 21–22.

Appendix

Altering the Default Setting

Re-envisaging the Early Transmission of the Jesus Tradition

Defining a Default Setting

For some time now I have been reflecting on the perils of "the default setting." For any who may be less than familiar with the pleasures and perils of computers or of word processing, let me explain. From my *Idiot's Guide to the One-Eyed Monster* I read this definition: "Default is a pre-set preference that is used by a program, the 'fallback' position." In word processing, for

The presidential address at the 57th Annual Meeting of Studiorum Novi Testamenti Societas at the University of Durham, August 6–10, 2002. I wish to acknowledge my debt to Annekie Joubert for advice on current research into oral culture in southern Africa, and to Werner Kelber for several helpful comments on an earlier draft of the paper, but particularly also to Terence Mournet, who for nearly three years worked closely with me on the theme of oral tradition in the Gospels. Not only has he provided invaluable advice on bibliography and the PowerPoint oral presentation of the "live" paper, but also several of the insights and observations developed in the paper are the outcome of our joint deliberations over the past two years. An earlier version of this essay appeared in *New Testament Studies* 49 (2003): 139–75, and is used by permission.

example, there may be a default setting for the style of type and size of font used—let us say, New York type, 12-point size; also for margins of a certain width—let us say, 2 inches.

The problems come when you want to change your default settings. You may want a broader margin (2.5 inches) and to use Palatino type in 10-point size. And so you set up all these different options; you format the document you are writing according to your own design, and override the default settings provided for you by your computer or program. All that is fine, and you produce the document according to your preferred format. The trouble is that when you open a *new* document and want to start afresh, you find that, whether you wanted to or not, your format has reverted to the original default settings.

The default setting means that when you want to create something different, you need constantly to resist the default setting, you need consciously to change or alter it. But when you turn your attention elsewhere, the default setting, the preset preference, reasserts itself.[1]

The default setting is a useful image to remind us of our own preset preferences, the mind-set by which we unconsciously, instinctively process and format information. The most obvious example today is the difficulty which many (most) of my generation in Britain have in dealing with centimeters and liters. *Inches* and *feet* and *pints* are so deeply bred into us that we automatically think in these terms. They are our default settings. I *think* inches; I do not think centimeters. And when confronted with centimeters, I must consciously revise my way of looking at the item in question.

Similarly, perhaps, with languages. Many people are fluent in several languages. But the first language, the language of childhood, is likely to be the default language. In moments of stress or great emotion, our involuntary reflex is to speak in our mother tongue.

The more serious examples are the default settings that determine our attitudes and behavior toward others. Through the nineteenth and most of the twentieth centuries, the idea of

---

1. On a computer, of course, the experienced operator can easily alter the default setting. My point is that it is much more difficult to alter the default setting of the "onboard mental computer." The analogy is not precise!

progress was a default setting. It was the way European academics saw history and the historical role of the West. That is, we understood progress as scientific advance, as the spread of European "civilization." The consequences are still a major factor in our relationships with Africa and the Far East.

In Britain the mistakes made in investigating the tragic murder of a black London teenager in 1993 forced us to confront the reality of what the official report, the Macpherson Report, described as "institutional racism."[2] "Institutional racism" is Macpherson's term for a prejudicial mind-set toward individuals of another race, which unconsciously predetermines attitudes and actions in particular instances. "Institutional racism," in other words, is another example of a default setting—an involuntary reflex attitude, a "preset preference" in attitudes endemic within, in the case in point, the Metropolitan Police force. The point is not to deny that such attitudes were being combated, not to deny that when members of the Metropolitan Police concentrated on the problem they succeeded in avoiding racist sentiments. The point rather is that when people did *not* concentrate on the problem, when they relaxed their vigilance, they fell back to their default setting; their actions expressed their involuntary preset preferences.

So too in Christian circles and in NT scholarship, it is only relatively recently that we have become aware of the default setting of centuries-old *patriarchalism*. We simply took it for granted, as an unexamined a priori, that "man" of course denotes humanity, that "brethren/brothers" of course is an appropriate way to address a Christian congregation. I recall the shock I experienced when working on Romans 16 to find commentators convinced that προστάτις (*prostatis*) in 16:2 could mean only something like "helper" (RSV), because, of course, a woman (Phoebe) could not have been a "patron," the normal meaning of the word προστάτις. Likewise, the accusative Ἰουνιᾶν must denote a man, Junias rather than Junia, because, of course, a woman could not have been "outstanding among the apostles"

2. The Macpherson Report on *The Stephen Lawrence Inquiry* (London: Stationery Office, 1999) identifies "institutional racism" in "processes, attitudes and behavior which amount to discrimination through unwitting prejudice, ignorance, thoughtlessness and racist stereotyping which disadvantages minority ethnic people" (28).

(16:7).[3] Was such logic not indicative of a patriarchalist mind-set or default setting?

If anything, more serious has been what might be called "the institutional anti-Semitism," or more accurately anti-Judaism, which for so long disfigured Christian theology, including NT scholarship. What was it that caused our predecessors to perse-vere with a description of Second Temple Judaism as *"late* Juda-ism," *Spätjudentum,* well into the second half of the twentieth century? They must have been aware that such a description perpetuated Christian supersessionism, the belief that Judaism's only function was to prepare for Christianity. This implies that when Christianity came Judaism ceased to have a reason for existence, and that first-century Judaism was *late* Judaism, the *last* Judaism. Such a supersessionist attitude must have become so inbred over centuries, an involuntary reflex, a subconscious default setting, that our predecessors fell back to it without thinking.

A default setting, then, a computer's preset preferences, is a useful image of an established mind-set, an unconscious bias or *Tendenz,* an instinctive reflex response. The point is that to alter a default setting, to change a habitual attitude or instinc-tive perspective, requires a conscious and sustained or repeated effort, otherwise without realizing it we revert to the default setting, to our unexamined predispositions.

However, it is another default setting in NT scholarship that I want to speak about in this essay.

The Literary Paradigm

We are all children of Gutenberg and Caxton. We belong to cultures shaped by the book. Our everyday currency is the learned article and monograph. Libraries are our natural habi-tat. We trace the beginnings of our modern discipline to the Renaissance's reassertion of the importance of studying classical texts in their original languages, to Erasmus's first Greek New Testament in 1516. Our discipline developed in the nineteenth

3. For details, see my *Romans,* WBC 38 (Dallas: Word, 1988), 888–89, 894–95.

century around the distinction between "lower criticism" (the attempt to reconstruct the original text of our NT writings) and "higher criticism" (concerned with questions of sources and genre). The dominant mode of treating the Synoptic Gospels during the last generation has been redaction criticism, the Gospels as the product of literary editing. Today a major concern for many is summed up in the word "intertextuality," where the appropriation of earlier texts, oral as well as written, is conceived in exclusively literary terms.

In a word, we naturally, habitually, and instinctively work within a *literary paradigm*. We are, therefore, in no fit state to appreciate how a *non*literary culture, an *oral* culture, functions. And if we are to enter empathetically into such a culture, it is essential that we become conscious of our literary paradigm and make deliberate efforts to step outside it and to free ourselves from its inherited predispositions. It becomes necessary to alter the default settings given by the literary-shaped software of our mental computers.

The prevalence of the literary paradigm in study of the Synoptic tradition can be readily illustrated, as also the fact that it has both shaped and restricted NT scholarship's way of envisaging the Jesus tradition and its early transmission.

I need only remind you of the eighteenth- and nineteenth-century debate about the origins of the Synoptic tradition.[4] The early solution of G. E. Lessing and J. G. Eichhorn was of an original gospel composed in Aramaic, written as early as 35, and known to the three Synoptic evangelists in different recensions.[5]

---

4. Of the various reviews and analyses, I found the following most helpful: T. Zahn, *Introduction to the New Testament*, 3 vols. (Edinburgh: Clark, 1909), 2:400–427; J. Moffatt, *An Introduction to the Literature of the New Testament* (Edinburgh: Clark, 1911; 3rd ed., 1918), 179–217; W. G. Kümmel, *Introduction to the New Testament* (1973; ET: London: SCM, 1975), 44–80; B. Reicke, *The Roots of the Synoptic Gospels* (Philadelphia: Fortress, 1986), ch. 1; E. P. Sanders and M. Davies, *Studying the Synoptic Gospels* (London: SCM, 1989), 51–162; U. Schnelle, *The History and Theology of the New Testament Writings* (ET: London: SCM, 1998), 162–97; J. S. Kloppenborg Verbin, *Excavating Q: The History and Setting of the Sayings Gospel* (Minneapolis: Fortress, 2000), 271–408.

5. For G. E. Lessing, see his "Neue Hypothese über die Evangelisten," in *Theologiekritische Schriften I und II*, vol. 7 of *Werke* (Munich: Hanser, 1976), 614–36; ET: *Theological Writings: Selections in Translation*, with introductory essay by H. Chadwick (London: Black, [1956]). W. G. Kümmel, *The New Testament: The His-*

Schleiermacher's "fragment hypothesis" was conceived in terms of multiple written sources, on which various recollections, notes, or reports of Jesus had been written.[6] It is true that Herder and Gieseler thought more in terms of an orally formulated tradition; though Herder was evidently still thinking of a full gospel, "a history of Christ";[7] and Gieseler assumed that frequent repetition produced a fixed form of the narrative and outline of Gospel history from the Baptist onward, in which the most important events and sayings were reproduced with great uniformity, so that this Gospel survived, in spite of modifications, in its original stereotyped form.[8]

Such alternatives, however, were swamped by the dominant impression that "the Synoptic Problem" could be solved only in terms of literary sources, that the intricate variations and coincidences in the Synoptic Gospels could be realistically explained only in terms of literary dependence. As James Moffatt summed up the nineteenth-century debate:

> The gospels are books made out of books; none of them is a document which simply transcribes the oral teaching of an apostle or of apostles. Their agreements and differences cannot be explained except on the hypothesis of a more or less close literary relationship, and while oral tradition is a *vera causa*, it is only a subordinate factor in the evolution of our canonical Greek gospels.[9]

It should occasion no surprise, then, that the hypothesis that emerged in the late-nineteenth and early-twentieth centuries as the most plausible resolution of the Synoptic Problem is

---

tory of the Investigation of Its Problems (2nd ed., 1970; ET: Nashville: Abingdon, 1972), provides extensive excerpts from both Lessing and Eichhorn (76–79). See also Zahn, *Introduction*, 2:403–4; Schnelle, *History*, 162–63.

6. Reicke, *Roots*, 12–13, refers to F. Schleiermacher, *Über die Schriften des Lukas: Ein kritischer Versuch* (Berlin: Reimer, 1817), fifteen years before the better known "Über die Zeugnisse des Papias von unseren beiden ersten Evangelien," *Theologische Studien und Kritiken* 5 (1832): 738–58.

7. J. G. Herder, "Vom Erlöser der Menschen," *Herder Werke: Theologische Schriften* 9/1 (Frankfurt: Deutscher Klassiker, 1994), particularly 671–87, here 679; see also Reicke, *Roots*, 9–12.

8. I echo Zahn's description (*Introduction*, 2:409).

9. Moffatt, *Introduction*, 180.

still known simply as the two-*document* hypothesis.[10] And even
when some variations are offered in explanation of some of the
complexities of the data, like *Ur-Markus* or Proto-Luke, what is
envisaged are still *written* documents.[11] The literary paradigm
continues to determine the way the problem and its solution
are conceptualized. B. H. Streeter certainly recognized the importance of "a living oral tradition" behind the Gospels and
cautioned against studying the Synoptic Problem "merely as
a problem of literary criticism," but, ironically, he went on to
develop "a *four document* hypothesis."[12]

The main development from and challenge to *source* criticism was, of course, *form* criticism, which began as a deliberate attempt to break away from the literary paradigm and
to conceptualize the transmission process in oral terms. The
character of the challenge was already signaled by Wellhausen's
observation: "Die letzte Quelle der Evangelien ist mündliche
Überlieferung, aber diese enthält nur den zerstreuten Stoff."[13]
In effect, Wellhausen was combining the hypotheses of Herder
and Schleiermacher—Jesus tradition as oral tradition but in
small units. Bultmann took up the challenge when he defined
the purpose of form criticism thus: "to study the history of the
oral tradition behind the gospels."[14] His analysis of *The History
of the Synoptic Tradition*, I need hardly remind you, became the
single most influential exposition of *Formgeschichte*.[15]

Unfortunately, however, Bultmann could not escape from the
literary default setting; he could not conceive of the process of
transmission except in literary terms. This becomes most evident in his conceptualization of the whole tradition about Jesus

10. There is no need to rehearse the usual litany of Lachmann, Weisse, et
al.; for details, see, e.g., Kümmel, *New Testament*, 146–51; Kloppenborg Verbin,
Excavating Q, 295–309.

11. On *Ur-Markus*, see, e.g., Kümmel, *Introduction*, 61–63; and Proto-Luke,
particularly V. Taylor, *Behind the Third Gospel* (Oxford: Clarendon, 1926).

12. B. H. Streeter, *The Four Gospels: A Study of Origins* (London: Macmillan,
1924), ch. 9, quotations from 229.

13. J. Wellhausen, *Einleitung in die drei ersten Evangelien* (Berlin: Georg
Reimer, 1905), 43; English translation on 39, above.

14. R. Bultmann (with K. Kundsin), *Form Criticism* (1934; ET: New York:
Harper Torchbook, 1962), 1.

15. *Die Geschichte der synoptischen Tradition* (Göttingen: Vandenhoeck &
Ruprecht, 1921; ET: Oxford: Blackwell, 1963).

as "composed of a series of layers."[16] The imagined process is one where each layer is laid or builds upon another. Bultmann made such play with it because, apart from anything else, he was confident that he could strip off later (Hellenistic) layers to expose the earlier (Palestinian) layers.[17] The image itself, however, is drawn from the literary process of editing, where each successive edition (layer) is an edited version (for Bultmann, an elaborated and expanded version) of the previous edition (layer). But is such a conceptualization really appropriate to a process of *oral* retellings of traditional material? Bultmann never really addressed the question, despite its obvious relevance.

Similarly, Kümmel in his classic *Introduction* recognizes the importance of oral tradition, both in "fixing" the gospel material in written form and in the reworking of the earliest sources into the canonical Gospels; but his discussion focuses mainly on the two-source hypothesis, and his references to form-critical analyses do little to carry the discussion forward or to envisage how a process of oral transmission worked or how it might have influenced the shape of the tradition.[18] It may be true, as E. P. Sanders affirms, that "everyone accepts oral transmission at the early stages of the gospel tradition."[19] But in reality the role of oral tradition is either reduced to characteristically fragmentary forms[20] or unknown oral sources are postulated. In the latter case the working assumption, signaled by the word "source" itself, is usually that the source was in effect a fixed version of some Jesus tradition used by the evangelist as one would use a written document.[21]

16. R. Bultmann, *Jesus and the Word* (1926; ET: New York: Scribners, 1935), 12–13.

17. Ibid.

18. Kümmel, *Introduction*, particularly 76–79; Schnelle's acknowledgment of the role of oral tradition is cursory (*History*, 174).

19. Sanders and Davies, *Studying*, 141. Sanders and Davies, and Reicke (*Roots*), are fairly exceptional in the importance they have accorded to oral tradition in the development of the Jesus tradition.

20. ". . . those fragments of tradition that bear the imprint of orality: short, provocative, memorable, oft-repeated phrases, sentences, and stories" (R. W. Funk and R. W. Hoover, *The Five Gospels: The Search for the Authentic Words of Jesus* [New York: Macmillan/Polebridge, 1993], 4).

21. "Even now, when we have come to affirm that behind some or many of the literary works we deal with there is an oral tradition, we still manipulate such

Even more revealing are the various more-recent attempts to contest the dominance of the two-document hypothesis. W. Farmer's attempt to revive the Griesbach hypothesis (Luke dependent on Matthew, and Mark on both) only begins to make sense if the Synoptic Problem is viewed in exclusively literary terms, of one document dependent on and derived from another.[22] Sanders issued a justified critique of Bultmann's assumption of a uniform tendency in the development of the original "pure forms" of the Jesus tradition; yet his critique itself suffers from the idea of linear development evoked by the word "tendency."[23] M.-É. Boismard in turn assumes that the complexity of the Synoptic Problem can be resolved only by a complex literary solution, a multistage interaction among earlier and later versions of the three Synoptic Gospels.[24] M. D. Goulder demonstrates that once the hypothesis of literary dependence is given exclusive explanatory rights, then, with sufficient imagination and ingenuity, Matthew can be derived entirely from Mark, and Luke by a combination of the prior two.[25] And Mark Goodacre, despite acknowledging the potential importance of oral tradition, discusses individual cases in terms exclusively of literary dependence.[26]

At the present time the main focus of interest lies in Q. As the transition from the nineteenth to the twentieth century was dominated by fascination with the Gospel of Mark, so the tran-

---

traditions as though they too were 'literary' works" (W. H. Silberman, "'Habent Sua Fata Libelli': The Role of Wandering Themes in Some Hellenistic Jewish and Rabbinic Literature," in *The Relationships among the Gospels*, ed. W. O. Walker [San Antonio: Trinity University Press, 1978], 195–218, here 215).

22. W. R. Farmer, *The Synoptic Problem* (New York: Macmillan, 1964), ch. 6.

23. E. P. Sanders, *The Tendencies of the Synoptic Tradition*, SNTSMS 9 (Cambridge: Cambridge University Press, 1969).

24. M.-É. Boismard, "The Two-Source Theory at an Impasse," *New Testament Studies* 26 (1979): 261–73; also "Théorie des niveaux multiples," in *The Interrelations of the Gospels: A Symposium Led by M.-É. Boismard, W. R. Farmer, F. Neirynck, Jerusalem 1984*, ed. D. L. Dungan, BETL 95 (Leuven: Leuven University Press, 1990), 231–43. See also the discussion in Sanders and Davies, *Studying*, 105–11.

25. M. Goulder, *Luke: A New Paradigm*, 2 vols., JSNTSup 20 (Sheffield: Sheffield Academic Press, 1989), in his attempt to dispense with Q (particularly vol. 1, ch. 2).

26. M. Goodacre, *The Case against Q* (Harrisburg, PA: Trinity, 2002), 56–59, 89–90 (despite 64–66, 188).

sition from the twentieth to the twenty-first century has been
dominated by fascination with the second of the two sources in
the two-document hypothesis—the second source common to
Matthew and Luke, the sayings source Q. That Q was a document, written in Greek, is one of the principal points of consensus. Yet overdependence on the literary paradigm again dictates,
as with Mark and *Ur-Markus*, that divergences between Matthean
and Lukan Q material have to be explained by postulating different versions of Q, a Q^{Mt} and a Q^{Lk}.[27] The debate, however, now
focuses on the issue whether different compositional layers can
be distinguished *within* Q, with Kloppenborg's hypothesis that
three layers can be so discerned winning a substantial following.[28] What is of interest here is the almost explicit assumption
that each layer is to be conceived as a written document, and
the process of development conceived in terms of editing and
redaction. It should occasion no surprise that Kloppenborg envisages his investigation of Q in terms of an archaeological dig, as
Excavating Q, where, as with Bultmann, the process is visualized
as stripping away successive layers to reach the bottom layer,
or as removing the redactional elements of successive editions
to recover the original edition.[29]

Finally, we might simply note that the discussion of possible
knowledge of Jesus tradition in Paul's letters has similarly suffered
from an assumption that the case depends on a quasi-literary interdependency. Since the case cannot be clearly made that Paul knew
the form of tradition as it has been recorded in Mark or Q, the case
cannot be made for such interdependency.[30] That Paul, James, and
1 Peter, not to mention the Apostolic Fathers, bear testimony to
different versions of the *same* sayings of Jesus has been too little

27. E.g., Schnelle, *History*, 187.
28. J. S. Kloppenborg, *The Formation of Q: Trajectories in Ancient Wisdom
Collections* (Philadelphia: Fortress, 1987).
29. Kloppenborg does not explicitly address the issue of whether Q^1 was also
a document, but he does assume it (*Excavating Q*, 159, 197, 200, 208–9); see
also 154–59 on the genre of Q^1.
30. Notably F. Neirynck, "Paul and the Sayings of Jesus," in *L'Apôtre Paul*, ed.
A. Vanhoye, BETL 73 (Leuven: Peeters, 1986), 265–321; reprinted in *Evangelica*,
vol. 2, ed. F. van Segbroeck (Leuven: Peeters, 1991), 511–68. Neirynck's many
and valuable contributions on the Gospels well illustrate the dominance of the
literary paradigm.

considered. More to the point, such allusions to what we know from the Synoptics as Jesus tradition attest a much more diverse and fluid transmission process. This situation has been allowed too little say in our conceptualization of the character of the Jesus tradition and the way it was initially passed on.[31]

In all this discussion the literary paradigm has dominated. Even when a conscious effort has been made to alter the default setting, to recall that oral tradition would not necessarily move along the grooves of literary composition, of reading and revising, the literary paradigm soon reasserts its influence and closes down the historical possibilities that may be envisaged. As soon as attention shifts from the perspective itself to the data to be discussed, the default setting clicks back into place, and the interrelationships of the data are conceived in literary terms as though no other terms were relevant.

Should this be so? Need this be so?

What Do We Mean by an Oral Culture?

We should not underestimate the difficulty for a mind-set formed within a long-established literary culture trying to shift to an oral mind-set, the difficulty for someone bred to the literary paradigm trying to enter empathetically into an oral paradigm. Walter Ong effectively illustrates the problem by imagining how difficult it would be for those who knew only transport by automobile to visualize a *horse*, a horse conceptualized as an automobile without wheels.

> Imagine writing a treatise on horses (for people who have never seen a horse) which starts with the concept not of horse but of "automobile," built on the readers' direct experience of automobiles. It proceeds to discourse on horses by always referring to them as "wheelless automobiles," explaining to highly automobilized readers who have never seen a horse all the points of difference in an effort to excise all idea of "automobile" out of the concept of "wheelless

31. I of course except H. Koester, *Synoptische Überlieferung bei den apostolischen Vätern* (Berlin: Akademie-Verlag, 1957); also *Ancient Christian Gospels: Their History and Development* (London: SCM, 1980), 49–75; though Koester has not attempted to develop a model of oral transmission.

automobile" so as to invest the term with a purely equine meaning. Instead of wheels, the wheelless automobiles have enlarged toenails called hooves; instead of headlights or perhaps rear-vision mirrors, eyes; instead of a coat of lacquer, something called hair; instead of gasoline for fuel, hay; and so on. . . . No matter how accurate and thorough such apophatic description, automobile-driving readers who have never seen a horse and who hear only of "wheelless automobiles" would be sure to come away with a strange concept of a horse. . . . You cannot without serious and disabling distortion describe a primary phenomenon by starting with a subsequent secondary phenomenon and paring away the differences. Indeed, starting backwards in this way—putting the car before the horse—you can never become aware of the real differences at all.[32]

The uncomfortable fact is that if we are to accomplish such a paradigm switch, we probably need to be jolted out of the one and make a conscious and sustained effort to train our thinking to the other. If we are to begin to appreciate what it must have been like to live and function in an oral society, we must shake ourselves free from the unconscious presuppositions that shape the very way we see the Synoptic Problem and envisage the early transmission or retelling of the Jesus tradition.[33]

For a start we should recall the estimate of credible authorities that literacy in Palestine at the time of Jesus would probably have been less than 10 percent.[34] Given the importance of

32. W. J. Ong, *Orality and Literacy: The Technologizing of the Word* (London: Methuen, 1982; London and New York: Routledge, 1988), 12–13. See also M. McLuhan, *The Gutenberg Galaxy: The Making of Typographic Man* (Toronto: University of Toronto Press, 1962); and E. A. Havelock, *The Muse Learns to Write: Reflections on Orality and Literacy from Antiquity to the Present* (New Haven: Yale University Press, 1986), where Havelock sums up a scholarly lifetime of reflection on the transition from orality to literacy.

33. W. H. Kelber, *The Oral and the Written Gospel* (Philadelphia: Fortress, 1983; reprinted, Bloomington: Indiana University Press, 1996), begins with a similar protest (xv–xvi).

34. Recent estimates are of less than 10 percent literacy in the Roman Empire under the principate, falling to perhaps as low as 3 percent literacy in Roman Palestine; see particularly W. V. Harris, *Ancient Literacy* (Cambridge, MA: Harvard University Press, 1989); M. Bar-Ilan, "Illiteracy in the Land of Israel in the First Centuries CE," in *Essays in the Social Scientific Study of Judaism and Jewish Society*, ed. S. Fishbane and S. Schoenfeld (Hoboken, NJ: Ktav, 1992), 46–61; C. Hezser, *Jewish Literacy in Roman Palestine* (Tübingen: Mohr Siebeck, 2001).

Torah learning in Jewish culture, that estimate can be questioned. But given equally that royal officials, priests, scribes, and Pharisees would have made up a significant portion of the 10 percent, the corollaries are probably much the same. These corollaries include the fact that knowledge of Torah for most people would have been by *hearing*, aural, rather than by reading. We have to assume, therefore, that the great majority of Jesus' first disciples would have been functionally illiterate.[35] That Jesus himself was literate cannot simply be assumed.[36] And even allowing for the possibility that one or two of Jesus' immediate disciples were able to read and write (Matthew) and may even have kept notes of Jesus' teaching,[37] it remains *overwhelmingly probable that the earliest transmission of the Jesus tradition was by word of mouth*.[38] This also means, as Herder and the early form critics appreciated, that the forms of the tradition were already becoming *established* in *oral* usage and transmission.

Second, we need to recall the character of rural Galilee, where, on almost any reckoning, the initial impulse that resulted in the Jesus tradition is to be located. We can be confident that the village and small-town culture within which Jesus predominantly operated and where the stories and teachings of Jesus were first retold was a predominantly oral culture. Through recent archaeological work in Galilee, we have a much better idea of the physical settings in which that early formulation of the Jesus

35. Kloppenborg Verbin properly reminds us that " 'literacy' itself admits of various levels: signature-literacy; the ability to read simple contracts, invoices and receipts; full reading literacy; the ability to take dictation; and scribal literacy—the ability to compose" (*Excavating Q*, 167).

36. J. D. Crossan, *The Birth of Christianity* (San Francisco: HarperSanFrancisco, 1998), has little doubt that Jesus was illiterate (235); similarly, B. Chilton, *Rabbi Jesus: An Intimate Biography* (New York: Doubleday, 2000), 99.

37. See, particularly, A. Millard, *Reading and Writing in the Time of Jesus*, Biblical Seminar 69 (Sheffield: Sheffield Academic Press, 2000), 223–29; also E. E. Ellis, *The Making of the New Testament Documents* (Leiden: Brill, 1999), 24, 32, 352.

38. Pace W. Schmithals, "Vom Ursprung der synoptischen Tradition," *Zeitschrift für Theologie und Kirche* 94 (1997): 288–316, who continues to argue that the Synoptic tradition was literary from the first. Ellis, *Christ and the Future in New Testament History*, NovTSup 97 (Leiden: Brill, 2000), 13–14, also queries whether there was an initial oral stage of transmission.

tradition took place.[39] Here a trite but necessary reminder is that in the first century there were no newspapers, no television, no radio. But have we done enough to think through what that must have meant for communities? In the villages and small towns of Galilee, when the day's work was over and the sun had set, what else was there to do but to sit round and talk, to share the news of the day, to tell stories, to recall matters of importance for the community? Kenneth Bailey suggests that the traditional evening gathering of Middle Eastern villagers to listen to and recite the tradition of the community, the *haflat samar*, is the continuation of a practice that stretches back to the time of Jesus and beyond.[40]

Can we say more about the character of oral tradition and about oral transmission? As Sanders points out, the problem is "that we do not know how to imagine the oral period."[41] In an overwhelmingly literary culture, our experience of orality is usually restricted to casual gossip and the serendipitous reminiscences of college reunions. The burden of my essay, however, is that we *must* endeavor to "imagine the oral period" for the sake of historical authenticity, to re-envisage how tradition was transmitted in an orally structured society; also, that we *can* do so, or at least are more able to do so than has generally been realized. Here we are in the fortunate position of being able to call upon a wide range of research into oral tradition. No longer is it a matter simply of depending on the research into the Homeric and Yugoslavian sagas by Milman Parry and Albert Lord.[42] But I think also, in particular, of research into oral tradition in Africa[43] and the thirty years

39. See D. R. Edwards and C. T. McCollough, eds., *Archaeology and the Galilee,* South Florida Studies in the History of Judaism 143 (Atlanta: Scholars, 1997); and particularly J. L. Reed, *Archaeology and the Galilean Jesus* (Harrisburg, PA: Trinity, 2000).

40. K. E. Bailey, "Informal Controlled Oral Tradition and the Synoptic Gospels," *Asia Journal of Theology* 5 (1991): 34–54; also "Middle Eastern Oral Tradition and the Synoptic Gospels," *ExpTim* 106 (1995): 363–67.

41. Sanders and Davies, *Studying,* 141; ironically, in the same volume Sanders has demonstrated that there is an equal problem, too little recognized, of "imagining the literary period."

42. The work of A. B. Lord, *The Singer of Tales* (Cambridge, MA: Harvard University Press, 1978), has been seminal, here especially ch. 5.

43. I refer particularly to J. Vansina, *Oral Tradition as History* (Madison: University of Wisconsin Press, 1985), a revision of his earlier *Oral Tradition: A Study*

of personal experience of Bailey in the Middle East, recorded as anecdotes.[44]

On the basis of such research it is possible to draw up a list of characteristic features of oral tradition. The point, I will stress at once and will no doubt need to stress repeatedly, is not that an oral tradition once recorded or transcribed will necessarily look any different from a literary tradition. Transcribed oral tradition and literary tradition, not altogether surprisingly, look very much the same. My point is rather to bring home the danger of *envisaging* the process of tradition transmission in too exclusively literary terms and to suggest that it will be necessary for us deliberately to alter our print-determined default setting when we try to envisage the early transmission of the Jesus tradition.

There are five characteristic features of oral transmission of tradition that deserve attention.

First, and most obvious—or should be most obvious—an *oral performance* is *not* like reading a literary text.[45] In reading a text it is possible to look back a few pages to check what was written earlier. Having read the text, you can take it with you and read it again later. A written text can be revised, or edited, and so on. But none of that is possible with an oral tradition. An oral performance is evanescent. It is an event. It happens and then is gone. Oral tradition is not *there* for the auditor to check back a few pages, or to take away, or to edit and revise. It is not a thing, an artifact like a literary text. That fact alone should be sufficient to cause us to question whether models of literary editing, intertextual dependence, or of archaeological layers are appropriate as we attempt to re-envisage the early transmission of the Jesus tradition.

---

in Historical Methodology (London: Routledge & Kegan Paul, 1965); R. Finnegan, *Oral Literature in Africa* (Oxford: Clarendon, 1970); and I. Okpewho, *African Oral Literature: Backgrounds, Character and Continuity* (Bloomington: Indiana University Press, 1992). Annekie Joubert notes that a paradigm shift took place in folklore studies in the late 1970s and early 1980s, when a new emphasis on performance directed attention away from the study of the formal patterning and symbolic content of the texts to the emergence of verbal art in the social interaction between performers and audiences—quoting from R. Bauman and C. L. Briggs, "Poetics and Performance as Critical Perspectives on Language and Social Life," *Annual Review of Anthropology* 19 (1990): 59–88, here 59–60.

44. See above, n40.

45. See, e.g., Finnegan, *Oral Literature,* 2–7.

Nor should we forget that even written documents like Paul's letters would not have been *read* by more than a very few. For the great majority of recipients, the letter would have been *heard* rather than read. And the public reading of the text would require careful preparation and practice if it was to be heard meaningfully. The public reading of such a letter, in other words, would itself have the character of a performance.[46] Which also means that general knowledge of and even reference back to such texts would depend much more on recollection of what had been heard when the text was read to the congregation than on an individual perusal of the text itself. In technical terms, oral tradition includes the phenomenon of *second orality*, that is, a written text known only through oral performance of the text.

Second, oral tradition is essentially *communal* in character. On the literary paradigm we envisage an author writing for a reader. We speak of the intended reader, the ideal reader, the implied reader. We envisage the characteristic context of communication as the individual reader poring over the text, as the text there on a shelf to be consulted by readers functioning as individuals in separate one-to-one encounters with the text. But oral tradition continues in existence because there are communities for whom the tradition is important. The tradition is performed with greater or less regularity (depending on its importance) in the gatherings of the community, kept alive for the community by the elders, teachers, or those acknowledged as proficient performers of the tradition.[47]

46. The point is well made by W. Dabourne, *Purpose and Cause in Pauline Exegesis*, SNTSMS 104 (Cambridge: Cambridge University Press, 1999), ch. 8. See further P. J. Achtemeier, "*Omne verbum sonat*: The New Testament and the Oral Environment of Late Western Antiquity," *Journal of Biblical Literature* 109 (1990): 3–27.

47. The point was never adequately worked through by the early form critics. The model of "oral history" drawn into the discussion by S. Byrskog, *Story as History—History as Story: The Gospel Tradition in the Context of Ancient Oral History*, WUNT 123 (Tübingen: Mohr Siebeck, 2000), while valuable in other aspects, also fails at this point. Oral history envisages tradition as elicited from eyewitnesses by a historian some years or decades later, tradition that might have been latent or only casually exchanged in the meantime. But the oral tradition model put forward here, in contrast, envisages a tradition that sustained a community through its regular performance. Byrskog, in fact, has no real conception of or indeed role for oral transmission as itself a bridging factor between past and present.

The recognition of this point has enabled J. M. Foley in recent years to merge oral tradition theory fruitfully with receptionalist literary theory. For it is precisely the communal character of oral tradition, the degree to which the elders or teachers retain the tradition on behalf of the community and the performers perform it for the benefit of the community, that reminds us of the community's role in such performances. The performer's awareness that some tradition is already familiar to the community is a factor in the performance. The performance is heard within the community's "horizons of expectation." The performance's "gaps of indeterminacy" can be filled out from the audience's prior knowledge of the tradition or of like traditions. What Foley calls the "metonymic reference" of a performance enables the performer to use a whole sequence of allusions to the community's store of tradition and enables the community thus to recognize the consistency of the performance with the whole.[48]

Third, as already implied, in the oral community there would be one or more who were recognized as having *primary responsibility for maintaining and performing the community's tradition*—the singer of tales, the bard, the elders, the teachers, the rabbis. An ancient oral society had no libraries or dictionaries or encyclopedias. It had instead to rely on individuals whose role in their community was to function as, in the words of Jan Vansina, "a walking reference library."[49] In NT terms this certainly accords with the role of the apostle in providing what can properly be called foundation tradition for the churches he founded.[50] And

48. J. M. Foley, *Immanent Art: From Structure to Meaning in Traditional Oral Epic* (Bloomington: Indiana University Press, 1991), chs. 1 and 2 (particularly 6–13 and 42–45); he is drawing on the language of H. R. Jauss and W. Iser. The argument is developed in J. M. Foley, *The Singer of Tales in Performance* (Bloomington: Indiana University Press, 1995), chs. 1–3. Foley's observation is also taken up by R. A. Horsley and J. A. Draper, *Whoever Hears You Hears Me: Prophets, Performance, and Tradition in Q* (Harrisburg, PA: Trinity, 1999), chs. 7–8. Annekie Joubert notes that "the use of allusion is normally an appeal to the audience to link the references, and the audience will have to draw on extra-performance/extra-textual information in order to interpret and to understand the web of allusive communication" (private correspondence).

49. Vansina, *Oral Tradition as History*, 37; similarly Havelock speaks of an oral "encyclopedia" of social habit and custom-law and convention (*Muse*, 57–58).

50. As in 1 Cor. 11:2, 23; 15:1–3; Phil. 4:9; Col. 2:6–7; 1 Thess. 4:1; 2 Thess. 2:15; 3:6.

the prominence of teachers in the earliest communities[51] is best explained by the communities' reliance on them as repositories of community tradition.[52]

This in turn suggests that the teachers would be responsible for a body of teaching, presumably what Luke refers to as "the apostles' teaching" (Acts 2:42). There is no reason to conceive of this teaching as entirely fragmentary, a sequence of individual forms preserved randomly. In his paper on "The Gospels as Oral Traditional Literature," Albert Lord observes that "oral traditional composers think in terms of blocks and series of blocks of tradition."[53] The Synoptic tradition itself attests such groupings of parables (e.g., Mark 4:2–34) and miracle stories (4:35–5:43; 6:32–52), of Jesus' teaching on exorcism (3:23–29) or discipleship (8:34–37), of sequences of events such as a day in the life of Jesus (1:21–38), and so on.[54] Our knowledge of how oral tradition "works" elsewhere suggests that this would have been the pattern from earliest days, as soon as the stories and sayings of Jesus began to be valued by the groups of his followers.

Fourth, oral tradition subverts the idea(l) of an *"original"* version. With minds attuned to the literary paradigm, we envisage an original form, a first edition, from which all subsequent edi-

51. Acts 13:1; Rom. 12:7; 1 Cor. 12:28–29; Gal. 6:6; Eph. 4:11; Heb. 5:12; James 3:1; *Didache* 13.2; 15.1–2.

52. From what we know of more formal teaching in the schools, we can be sure that oral instruction was the predominant means: "It is the 'living voice' of the teacher that has priority" (L. C. A. Alexander, "The Living Voice: Scepticism towards the Written Word in Early Christianity and in Graeco-Roman Texts," in *The Bible in Three Dimensions: Essays in Celebration of Forty Years of Biblical Studies in the University of Sheffield*, ed. D. J. A. Clines et al. [Sheffield: Sheffield Academic Press, 1990], 221–47, here 244).

53. A. B. Lord, "The Gospels as Oral Traditional Literature," in *Relationships*, ed. Walker, 33–91, here 59.

54. A fuller listing of such groupings of tradition would include the Beatitudes (Matt. 5:3, 4, 6, 11, 12//Luke 6:20b, 21b, 21a, 22, 23), the sequence of mini-parables in Mark 2:18–22 (followed by Matt. 9:14–17 and Luke 5:33–39), Jesus' responses to would-be disciples (Matt. 8:19–22//Luke 9:57–62), the cost of discipleship and danger of loss (Mark 8:34–38; again followed by Matt. 16:24–27 and Luke 9:23–26), the sayings about light and judgment in Mark 4:21–25 (followed by Luke 8:16–18), the "parables of crisis" (Matt. 24:42–25:13 pars.), Jesus and the Baptist (Matt. 11:2–19 par.), Jesus' teaching on his exorcisms (Matt. 12:24–45 pars.), and the sending out of the disciples on mission (Mark 6:7–13; Matt. 9:37–10:1, 7–16; Luke 9:1–6; 10:1–12).

tions can at least in principle be traced by form and redaction criticism. We envisage tradition-history as an archaeological tell where we can in principle dig through the layers of literary strata to uncover the original layer, the "pure form" of Bultmann's conceptualization of *Formgeschichte*. But in oral tradition each performance is not related to its predecessors or successors in that way. In oral tradition, as Lord particularly has observed, *each* performance is, properly speaking, an "original."[55]

The point here can easily be misunderstood or misrepresented, so let me elaborate it a little. As it applies to the Jesus tradition, the point is *not* that there was no originating impulse that gave birth to the tradition. In at least many cases we can be wholly confident that there were things Jesus said and did that made an *impact* on his disciples, a *lasting* impact. But properly speaking, the *tradition* of the event is not the *event* itself. And the *tradition* of the saying is not the *saying* itself. The tradition is at best the *witness* of the event, and as there were presumably several witnesses, so there may well have been several traditions, or versions of the tradition, *from the first*. We can speak of an originating *event*, but we should certainly hesitate before speaking of an original *tradition* of the event. The same is true even of a saying of Jesus. The tradition of the saying attests the impact made by the saying on one or more of the original audience. But it may well have been heard slightly differently by others of that audience, and so told and retold in different versions *from the first*. And if, as Kelber points out, Jesus himself used his most effective parables and aphorisms on more than one occasion, the ideal of a single original, authentic version once again reduces more to the figment of a literary-molded mind-set. Yes, we can and need to envisage

55. "In a sense each performance is 'an' original, if not 'the' original. The truth of the matter is that our concept of 'the original,' of 'the song,' simply makes no sense in oral tradition" (Lord, *Singer*, 100–101). R. Finnegan, *Oral Poetry: Its Nature, Significance and Social Context* (Cambridge: Cambridge University Press, 1977), also glosses Lord—"There is no correct text, no idea that one version is more 'authentic' than another: each performance is a unique and original creation with its own validity" (65)—and credits Lord with bringing this point home most convincingly (79). Kelber already took up the point: "Each oral performance is an irreducibly unique creation"; if Jesus said something more than once there is no "original" (*Oral*, 29, also 59, 62).

teaching that originated with Jesus, actions that characterized his mission. But to treat the history of the Jesus tradition as though it were a matter of recovering some *original version of the tradition* is to conceptualize the transmission of the Jesus tradition at best misleadingly; the Jesus Seminar completely misjudged the character of the Jesus tradition at this point.[56] In oral tradition, performance variation is integral to and even definitive of the tradition.[57]

Fifth and finally, oral tradition is characteristically (I do not say distinctively) a combination of *fixity* and *flexibility*, of *stability* and *diversity*. The preceding characteristics could easily be taken to encourage the idea of oral tradition as totally flexible and variable. That would be a mistake. In oral tradition there is characteristically a tale to be told, a teaching to be treasured, in and through and precisely by means of the varied performances. Oral tradition is oral memory; its primary function is to preserve and recall what is of importance from the past. Tradition, more or less by definition, embodies the concern for continuity with the past, a past drawn upon but also enlivened that it might illuminate the present and future. In the words of E. A. Havelock, "Variability and stability, conservatism and creativity, evanescence and unpredictability all mark the pattern of

56. Funk and Hoover, *The Five Gospels*; also R. W. Funk, *The Acts of Jesus: The Search for the Authentic Deeds of Jesus* (San Francisco: Harper/Polebridge, 1998). To recognize that variation is integral to orality likewise undercuts much of the critical criteria (particularly "contradiction with other accounts"), used by H. Reimarus, D. F. Strauss, and their successors.

57. A. Dundes, *Holy Writ as Oral Lit: The Bible as Folklore* (Lanham, MD: Rowman & Littlefield, 1999), insists "upon 'multiple existence' and 'variation' as the two most salient characteristics of folklore" (18–19). The problem of deriving a text from the recollections of a performance is well illustrated by the play *Pericles*, attributed to Shakespeare (S. Wells and G. Taylor, eds., *The Oxford Shakespeare* [Oxford: Clarendon, 1988], 1037); see further J. Bate, *The Genius of Shakespeare* (London: Picador, 1997), 75–87 (I owe the latter reference to H. D. Betz). Nor should it be forgotten that NT textual criticism has to take account of the diverse ways in which the text was performed/used, read/heard in different churches; see particularly B. D. Ehrman, *The Orthodox Corruption of Scripture: The Effect of Early Christological Controversies on the Text of the New Testament* (Oxford: Oxford University Press, 1993); D. C. Parker, *The Living Text of the Gospels* (Cambridge: Cambridge University Press, 1997); E. J. Epp, "The Multivalence of the Term 'Original Text' in New Testament Textual Criticism," *Harvard Theological Review* 92 (1999): 245–81.

oral transmission"—the "oral principle of 'variation within the same.'"[58] It is this combination, reverting to our second point, that makes it possible for the community both to acknowledge its tradition and to delight in the freshness of the individual performance.

My basic thesis, then, is that a proper recognition of the characteristics of oral tradition, as just outlined, requires us to alter the default setting of our typically literary mind-set. To recognize that the early transmission of the Jesus tradition took place in an *oral culture* and as *oral tradition* requires us consciously to *resist* the involuntary predisposition to conceive that process in *literary* terms and consciously to *re-envisage* that process in *oral* terms.

I have no time here to develop the theoretical model further. Suffice it to say, the model takes up the best of the insights of the early form critics, while avoiding the false paths that the literary paradigm led them down. That is to say, the recognition of the *oral* and *communal* character of the early Jesus tradition should be retrieved from the confusion caused by an unjustifiably schematic conception of the development of the tradition from pure to complex form, from simple to elaborated form.[59] Likewise, the "oral principle of 'variation within the same'" tells more heavily than has hitherto been appreciated against the assumption of Bultmann and Käsemann[60] that there was a steady

58. Kelber, *Oral*, 33, 54; quoting E. A. Havelock, *Preface to Plato* (Cambridge, MA: Harvard University Press, 1963), 92, 147, 184, passim.

59. "Das . . . Kriterium der 'reinen Gattung' stellt eine Vermischung linguistischer und sprachhistorischer Kategorien dar, die einer heute überholten Auffassung der Sprachentwicklung zuzuweisen ist"—J. Schröter, *Erinnerung an Jesu Worte*, Wissenschaftliche Monographien zum Alten und Neuen Testament 76 (Neukirchen-Vluyn: Neukirchener Verlag, 1997), 59, also 141–42. See also G. Strecker, "Schriftlichkeit oder Mündlichkeit der synoptischen Tradition?" in *The Four Gospels, 1992: Festschrift Frans Neirynck*, ed. F. van Segbroeck et al., BETL 100 (Leuven: Leuven University Press, 1992), 1:159–72, here 161–62, with other bibliography in n6.

60. Bultmann, *History*, 127–28: "In the primitive community at Jerusalem the spirit of Jesus continued to be active, and his ethical teaching was progressively elaborated and expressed in utterances which were then transmitted as the sayings of Jesus himself" ("The New Approach to the Synoptic Problem" [1926]; ET: *Existence and Faith* [London: Collins Fontana, 1964], 42); E. Käsemann, "Is the Gospel Objective?" *Essays on New Testament Themes* (London: SCM, 1964), 48–62.

inflow of fresh material from prophetic utterances into the Jesus tradition in the pre–AD 70 period.[61] The model also recognizes the strengths of Birger Gerhardsson's response to Bultmann while, hopefully, avoiding its weaknesses.[62] That is to say, the oral tradition model recognizes that where an influential teacher was in view, there was bound to be a concern among his disciples to remember what he had taught them.[63] But it sees the more fundamental trait of oral tradition in terms of the combination of flexibility as well as fixity, so that the character of oral transmission is not adequately caught by the single term "memorization."[64] Bailey's intermediate model of *in*formal *controlled* tradition seems closer to the more broadly recognizable oral-tradition model than either Bultmann's informal *un*controlled model or Gerhardsson's *formal* controlled model.[65]

61. See further Dunn, *Jesus Remembered* (Grand Rapids: Eerdmans, 2002), #8.2.

62. B. Gerhardsson, *Memory and Manuscript: Oral Tradition and Written Transmission in Rabbinic Judaism and Early Christianity* (Lund: Gleerup, 1961).

63. Finnegan critiques Lord in pointing out that memorization also plays a part in oral tradition (*Oral Poetry*, 79, 86).

64. E.g., "The general attitude was that words and items of knowledge must be memorized: *tantum scimus, quantum memoria tenemus*" (Gerhardsson, *Memory*, 124); "Cicero's saying was applied to its fullest extent in Rabbinic Judaism: *repetitio est mater studiorum*. Knowledge is gained by repetition, passed on by repetition, kept alive by repetition. A Rabbi's life is one continual repetition" (*Memory*, 168). Sanders and Davies rightly observe that Gerhardsson tries to allow for the flexibility of verbal tradition (citing Gerhardsson, *The Gospel Tradition*, Coniectanea biblica: New Testament Series 15 [Lund: Gleerup, 1986], 39–40), but that even so the Synoptic data do not fit well with the model (*Studying*, 129–32). R. Riesner, *Jesus als Lehrer: Eine Untersuchung zum Ursprung der Evangelien-Überlieferung*, WUNT 7/2 (Tübingen: Mohr Siebeck, 1981), 65–67, 440–53, also emphasizes the role of learning by heart (*Auswendiglernen*) in Jesus' teaching. D. L. Balch, "The Canon: Adaptable and Stable, Oral and Written: Critical Questions for Kelber and Riesner," *Forum* 7.3–4 (1991): 183–205, criticizes Riesner for assuming "a print mentality" that was not true of "passing on tradition of great philosophers' teachings" (196–99). See also 44n31, above.

65. I might simply add that the appeal sometimes made, by Horsley in particular (*Whoever Hears You*, 98–103; also *Hearing the Whole Story: The Politics of Plot in Mark's Gospel* [Louisville: Westminster John Knox, 2001], 157–59), to James C. Scott's use of the distinction between the "great tradition" and the "little tradition" in a community—the great tradition as expressing the dominant and dominating ruling power, the little tradition as expressing the hidden but continuing values and concerns of the oppressed community—is of little relevance for us. It is used by Scott in reference to a colonialist situation

So then, in the light of these characteristics of oral tradition, how do we go about re-envisaging the early transmission of the Jesus tradition?

Re-envisaging the Early Transmission

The test of any theoretical model for the transmission of the Jesus tradition, of course, is how well it explains the data we have, how well it explains the character of the Jesus tradition as we know it. I believe the oral-tradition model passes that test with flying colors. But before illustrating the claim, I need to make three preliminary points.

First, there is no possibility of producing a knockdown argument. I cannot produce a sample from the Jesus tradition that is demonstrably oral rather than literary in character.[66] This, of course, is partly because the tradition as we now have it is in literary form. So, naturally, it is literary in character. But it is also true anyway that there are no distinctive characteristics of any particular sample of tradition that enable us to pronounce definitively "Oral and not literary."[67]

On the other hand, the observation cuts both ways. That is to say, we should not assume that simply because the tradition as we now have it is in literary form, therefore its current form is the outcome of a process conceived in purely literary terms. My challenge once again is for us to shake ourselves out of that literary mind-set and to attempt to revisualize the part

---

in Southeast Asia, which has little bearing on a Jewish Galilee ruled by a client Jewish king. And in the Jesus tradition, we have not so much the persistence of old tradition but the emergence of new tradition (even if much of it can be regarded as a reconfiguration of older tradition).

66. I recall that my doctor-father, C. F. D. Moule, in the mid-1960s challenged his Cambridge Seminar to produce such a knockdown example in regard to any solution of the Synoptic Problem; no example went unquestioned.

67. Note the conclusion of the symposium on *Jesus and the Oral Gospel Tradition*, ed. H. Wansbrough, JSNTSup 64 (Sheffield: Sheffield Academic Press, 1991): "We have been unable to deduce or derive any marks which distinguish clearly between an oral and a written transmission process. Each can show a similar degree of fixity and variability" (12). Strecker rightly emphasizes the continuity in transmission of the tradition from oral to written ("Schriftlichkeit," 164–65). Cf. Schröter, *Erinnerung*, 55, 60.

of the process that must have been largely if not entirely oral in character. What I ask for is that we seriously attempt to re-conceptualize the parameters and constraints within which we envisage the transmission of the Jesus tradition taking place. It is not *what* we look at, so much as the *way* we look at it, that we need to reflect on.

Second, as just implied, we simply cannot escape from a *presumption of orality* for the first stage of the transmission of the Jesus tradition. In a society that was so illiterate and where the great bulk of communication must have taken place in oral mode, it would be ludicrous either to assume that the whole history of the Jesus tradition was literary in character from start to finish or to make any thesis regarding the process of its transmission dependent in effect on such an assumption. I say this in response to various recent claims either that the Jesus tradition took literary form from the first,[68] or that all differences between parallel traditions, no matter how great, can be explained in terms of literary redaction.[69] As indicated earlier, I do not for a moment deny that differences within the Synoptic tradition *can* be explained in terms of the literary paradigm. My question is whether they *should* be so explained, and whether in so doing we do not lose sight of important features of the Jesus

68. See above, n38.
69. B. W. Henaut, *Oral Tradition and the Gospels: The Problem of Mark 4*, JSNTSup 82 (Sheffield: JSOT, 1993), is tendentiously concerned to argue the virtual impossibility of recovering any oral tradition behind the Gospels: all differences, no matter how great, can be explained in terms of literary redaction; and oral tradition was wholly fluid and contingent on the particularities of each performance. But his conception of the oral tradition process is questionable—as though it was a matter of recovering a history of tradition through a set of sequential performances (e.g., 118). And he gives too little thought to what the stabilities of oral remembrances of Jesus might be as distinct from those in the epics and sagas studied by Parry and Lord. H. W. Hollander, "The Words of Jesus: From Oral Tradition to Written Record in Paul and Q," *Novum Testamentum* 42 (2000): 340–57, follows Henaut uncritically (351–55): he has no conception of tradition as reflecting/embodying the impact of anything Jesus said or did; and he thinks of oral tradition as essentially casual, without any conception that tradition could have a role in forming community identity and thus be important to such communities. Similarly, Crossan seems to think of oral tradition principally in terms of individuals' casual recollection (*Birth of Christianity*, 49–93).

tradition, the way it was regarded and handled, and what that tells us about the earliest communities that preserved it.

Third, despite the cautionary note I am sounding, I remain convinced of the essential correctness of the two-document hypothesis. That is to say, the evidence continues to persuade me that Mark was the earliest of the Synoptic Gospels, and that there was a further document behind Matthew and Luke on which both drew (Q). The primary evidence is as it has always been: the closeness of verbal parallels between two or three of the three documents. When I look at such passages as Mark 8:34–37 and parallels (the cost of discipleship) and 13:28–32 and parallels (the parable of the fig tree),[70] the evidence forces me to the conclusion that these three versions of particular Jesus traditions are interdependent at the literary level. The evidence almost requires us to speak of sources, of sources already in Greek, of one serving as the source for the other, or of each drawing on a common literary source (the underlining indicating the extent of the agreement).

Matthew 16:24–26	Mark 8:34–37	Luke 9:23–25
[24]Then Jesus told	[34]And he called to him the multitude with	
his disciples,	his disciples, and said to them,	[23]And he said to all,
"If any man would come after me, let him deny himself and take up his cross and follow me. [25]For whoever would save his life will lose it, and whoever loses his life for my sake	"If any man would come after me, let him deny himself and take up his cross and follow me. [35]For whoever would save his life will lose it; and whoever loses his life for my sake and the gospel's	"If any man would come after me, let him deny himself and take up his cross daily and follow me. [24]For whoever would save his life will lose it; and whoever loses his life for my sake, he
will find it. [26]For what will it profit a man, if he gains the whole world and forfeits his life?	will save it. [36]For what does it profit a man, to gain the whole world and forfeit his life?	will save it. [25]For what does it profit a man if he gains the whole world and loses or forfeits himself?"

70. Full statistics in R. Morgenthaler, *Statistische Synopse* (Zürich and Stuttgart: Gotthelf, 1971), 239–43.

Matthew 16:24–26	Mark 8:34–37	Luke 9:23–25
Or what shall a man give in return for his life?"	[37]For what can a man give in return for his life?"	

Matthew 24:32–36	Mark 13:28–32	Luke 21:29–33
[32]"From the fig tree learn its lesson: as soon as its branch becomes tender and puts forth its leaves, you know that the summer is near. [33]So also, when you see all these things, you know that he is near, at the very gates. [34]Truly, I say to you, this generation will not pass away till all these things take place. [35]Heaven and earth will pass away, but my words will not pass away. [36]But of that day and hour no one knows, not even the angels of heaven, nor the Son, but the Father only."	[28]"From the fig tree learn its lesson: as soon as its branch becomes tender and puts forth its leaves, you know that the summer is near. [29]So also, when you see these things taking place, you know that he is near, at the very gates. [30]Truly, I say to you, this generation will not pass away before all these things take place. [31]Heaven and earth will pass away, but my words will not pass away. [32]But of that day or that hour no one knows, not even the angels in heaven, nor the Son, but only the Father."	[29]And he told them a parable: "Look at the fig tree, and all the trees; [30]as soon as they come out in leaf, you see for yourselves and know that the summer is already near. [31]So also, when you see these things taking place, you know that the kingdom of God is near. [32]Truly, I say to you, this generation will not pass away till all has taken place. [33]Heaven and earth will pass away, but my words will not pass away."

The Q material has similar parallels, such as the preaching of John the Baptist in Matt. 3:7–10//Luke 3:7–9, and the parable of the returning evil spirits in Matt. 12:43–45//Luke 11:24–26.[71]

71. Full statistics in ibid., 258–61.

Matthew 3:7–10	Luke 3:7–9
[7]But when he saw many of the Pharisees and Sadducees coming for baptism, he said to them, "You brood of vipers! Who warned you to flee from the wrath to come? [8]Bear fruit that befits repentance, [9]and do not presume to say to yourselves, 'We have Abraham as our father'; for I tell you, God is able from these stones to raise up children to Abraham. [10]Even now the axe is laid to the root of the trees; every tree therefore that does not bear good fruit is cut down and thrown into the fire."	[7]He said therefore to the multitudes that came out to be baptized by him, "You brood of vipers! Who warned you to flee from the wrath to come? [8]Bear fruits that befit repentance, and do not begin to say to yourselves, 'We have Abraham as our father'; for I tell you, God is able from these stones to raise up children to Abraham. [9]Even now the axe is laid to the root of the trees; every tree therefore that does not bear good fruit is cut down and thrown into the fire."

Matthew 12:43–45	Luke 11:24–26
[43]"When the unclean spirit has gone out of a man, he passes through waterless places seeking rest, but he finds none. [44]Then he says, 'I will return to my house from which I came.' And when he comes he finds it empty, swept, and put in order. [45]Then he goes and brings with him seven other spirits more evil than himself, and they enter and dwell there; and the last state of that man becomes worse than the first. So shall it be also with this evil generation."	[24]"When the unclean spirit has gone out of a man, he passes through waterless places seeking rest; and finding none he says, 'I will return to my house from which I came.' [25]And when he comes he finds it swept and put in order. [26]Then he goes and brings seven other spirits more evil than himself, and they enter and dwell there; and the last state of that man becomes worse than the first."

So, I have no problems in recognizing the probability of literary interdependence between the Synoptic Gospels. My question, once again, is whether the hypothesis of literary interdependence is sufficient to explain *all* the data of correlation between the Gospel traditions. My question is whether we should take such close parallels as the *norm* for explaining *all* parallels, whether we should simply extrapolate from such examples and conclude that all parallels are to be explained in the same way.

Consider the following cases. As you look at these passages, I ask you to consider whether literary dependence is the only or most obvious explanation for the degree of similarity between the different versions.

1. *The triple tradition.* In the triple tradition consider first the account of the epileptic boy in Mark 9:14–27 and parallels. Note the cluster of agreement at vv. 18–19, 25, evidently the core of the story, and the wide variation for the rest (again, the underlining indicating the extent of the agreement).

Matthew 17:14–18	Mark 9:14–27	Luke 9:37–42
		[37]On the next day,
[14]And when they <u>came</u> to the	[14]And when they <u>came</u> to the disciples, they saw	when they had <u>come</u> down from the mountain,
<u>crowd,</u>	<u>a great crowd</u> about them, and scribes arguing with them. [15]And immediately all the crowd, when they saw him, were greatly amazed, and ran up to him and greeted him. [16]And he asked them, "What are you discussing with them?"	<u>a great crowd</u> met him.
<u>a man</u>	[17]And one of <u>the crowd</u>	[38]And behold, <u>a man</u> from <u>the crowd</u>
came up to him and kneeling before him said, [15]"Lord, have mercy on	answered him, "<u>Teacher,</u> I brought	cried, "<u>Teacher,</u> I beg you to look upon
<u>my son,</u> for he is an epileptic and he suffers terribly;	<u>my son</u> to you, for he has a dumb	<u>my son,</u> for he is my only child; [39]and behold, a
for often he falls into the fire, and often into the water.	<u>spirit;</u> [18]and wherever it grabs <u>him,</u> it dashes him down;	<u>spirit</u> seizes <u>him,</u> and he suddenly cries out; it convulses him
	and he foams and grinds his teeth and becomes rigid;	till he foams, and shatters him, and will hardly leave him.
[16]<u>And I</u> brought him to <u>your disciples,</u>	<u>and I</u> asked <u>your disciples to cast it out,</u>	[40]<u>And I</u> begged <u>your disciples to cast it out,</u>
<u>and</u> they could <u>not</u> heal him."	<u>and</u> they were <u>not</u> able."	<u>and</u> they could <u>not.</u>"

Matthew 17:14–18	Mark 9:14–27	Luke 9:37–42
[17]And Jesus answered, "O faithless and perverse generation, how long am I to be with you? How long am I to put up with you? Bring him here to me."	[19]And he answered them, "O faithless generation, how long am I to be with you? How long am I to put up with you? Bring him to me." [20]And they brought the boy to him; and when the spirit saw him, immediately it convulsed the boy, and he fell on the ground and rolled about, foaming at the mouth. . . . . [25]And when Jesus saw that a crowd came running together, he rebuked the unclean spirit, saying to it, "You dumb and deaf spirit, I command you, come out of him, and never enter him again." [26]And after crying out and convulsing him terribly, it came out, and the boy was like a corpse; so that most of them said, "He is dead." [27]But Jesus took him by the hand and lifted him up, and he arose.	[41]Jesus answered, "O faithless and perverse generation, how long am I to be with you and to put up with you? Lead your son here." [42]While he was coming, the demon tore him and convulsed him.

But Jesus rebuked the unclean spirit,

and healed the boy, and gave him back to his father. [43]And all were astonished at the majesty of God. |
[18]And Jesus rebuked him,		
and the demon came out of him,		
and the boy was cured from that hour.		

Or again, note the variations in the accounts of finding the empty tomb—Mark 16:1–8 and parallels.

Matthew 28:1–8	Mark 16:1–8	Luke 24:1–11
¹Now after the sabbath, toward the dawn of the first day of the week, Mary Magdalene and the other Mary	¹And when the sabbath was past,	¹But on the first day of the week, at early dawn,
	Mary Magdalene, and Mary the mother of James, and Salome, bought spices, so that they might go and anoint him. ²And very early on the first day of the week	
went to see the sepulcher.	they went to the tomb	they went to the tomb,
	when the sun had risen.	taking the spices which they had prepared.
²And behold, there was a great earthquake; for an angel of the Lord descended from heaven and came and	³And they were saying to one another, "Who will roll away the stone for us from the door of the tomb?" ⁴And looking up, they saw that	
		²And they found
rolled back the stone, and sat upon it.	the stone was rolled away—it was very large.	the stone rolled back from the tomb,
	⁵And entering the tomb,	³but when they entered
		they did not find the body. ⁴While they were perplexed about this, behold, two men stood by them in dazzling apparel;
³His appearance was like lightning, and his raiment white as snow. ⁴And for fear of him the guards trembled and became like dead men.	they saw a young man sitting on the right side, dressed in a white robe; and they were amazed.	⁵and as they were frightened and bowed their faces to the ground,
⁵But the angel said to the women, "Do not be afraid; for I know that you seek Jesus who was crucified.	⁶And he said to them, "Do not be amazed; you seek Jesus of Nazareth, who was crucified.	the men said to them, "Why do you seek the living among the dead?

Matthew 28:1-8	Mark 16:1-8	Luke 24:1-11
⁶He is not here; for he has risen, as he said. Come, see the place where he lay. ⁷Then go quickly and tell his disciples that he has risen from the dead, and behold,	He has risen, he is not here; see the place where they laid him. ⁷But go, tell his disciples and Peter that	
		⁶Remember how he told you, while he was still in Galilee, ⁷that the Son of man must be delivered into the hands of sinful men, and be crucified, and on the third day rise." ⁸And they remembered his words,
he is going before you to Galilee; there you will see him. Lo, I have told you."	he is going before you to Galilee; there you will see him, as he told you."	
⁸So they departed quickly from the tomb with fear and great joy,	⁸And they went out and fled from the tomb; for trembling and astonishment had come upon them;	⁹and returning from the tomb
and ran to tell his disciples.		they told all this to the Eleven and to all the rest.
	and they said nothing to anyone, for they were afraid.	
		¹⁰Now it was Mary Magdalene and Joanna and Mary the mother of James and the other women with them who told this to the apostles; ¹¹but these words seemed to them an idle tale, and they did not believe them.

My question is whether such evidence is not better explained in terms of *oral* tradition—that is, as *retellings* of a familiar story, with variations dependent on the teller's foibles and the community's perceived interests. That may mean that Matthew or Luke already knew versions of the stories that differed from Mark's, and that they followed these different versions. Or, bearing in mind the characteristics of oral performance, perhaps we should envisage Matthew and Luke *retelling* the story known to them from Mark, that is, retelling it *in oral mode*—as story tellers, rather than editors—with Matthew and Luke as evidence not so much of redaction as of second orality.

2. *The Q tradition?* The Q hypothesis, which I accept, is built in the first instance on the closeness of parallel between non-Markan pericopes in Matthew and Luke. More than 13 percent of these common pericopes are more than 80 percent in verbal agreement. But the fact that the verbal agreement in over a third of the common material is less than 40 percent[72] has not been given sufficient weight. Is it to be explained solely in terms of free redaction? Consider the following examples: turning the other cheek, in Matt. 5:39b–42//Luke 6:29–30; dividing families, in Matt. 10:34–38//Luke 12:51–53 and 14:26–27; and forgiving sins seven times, in Matt. 18:15, 21–22//Luke 17:3–4 (the underlining once again indicating the extent of the verbal agreement).

Matthew 5:39b–42	Luke 6:29–30
[39b]"But whoever hits you on your right <u>cheek,</u> turn to him <u>the other also;</u> [40]and to the one who wants to sue you and take your <u>tunic,</u> let him have your <u>cloak also;</u> [41]and whoever forces you to go one mile, go with him a second. [42]<u>Give to</u> the one <u>who asks you,</u> and do not turn away the one who wants to borrow from you."	[29]"To the one who strikes you on the <u>cheek,</u> offer <u>the other also;</u> and from the one who takes away your <u>cloak</u> do not withhold your <u>tunic also.</u> [30]<u>Give to</u> everyone <u>who asks you;</u> and from the one who takes what is yours, do not ask for them back."

72. See Kloppenborg Verbin's summary of Morgenthaler's data (*Excavating Q*, 63). In such cases, Kloppenborg Verbin defends a literary dependence by pointing out that Matthew and Luke show equal freedom in their use of Mark (64). But he does not consider the obvious alternative noted above, that such divergences of Matthew and Luke from Mark may indicate rather that Matthew and Luke knew and preferred to use other oral versions of the tradition, or to retell Mark's version in oral mode.

Matthew 10:34–38	Luke 12:51–53; 14:26–27
[34]"Do not think that I came to bring <u>peace</u> to <u>the earth</u>; I came not to bring peace, <u>but</u> a sword.	[12:51]"Do you consider that I am here to give <u>peace</u> on <u>the earth</u>? No, I tell you, <u>but</u> rather division! [52]From now on five in one household will be divided; three against two and two against three
[35]For I came to set a man against his <u>father</u>,	[53]they will be divided, father against son and son against <u>father</u>, mother against daughter
and a <u>daughter</u> against her <u>mother</u>,	and <u>daughter</u> against <u>mother</u>, mother-in-law against her daughter-in-law
and a <u>daughter-in-law</u> against her <u>mother-in-law</u>; [36]and a man's foes will be members of his own household.	and <u>daughter-in-law</u> against <u>mother-in-law</u>."
	. . . .
[37]Whoever loves <u>father</u> or <u>mother</u> more than me is not worthy of me; and whoever loves son or daughter more than me is not worthy of me;	[14:26]"Whoever comes to me and does not hate his <u>father</u> and <u>mother</u>, and wife and children, and brothers and sisters, yes, and even his own life, cannot be my disciple.
[38]and he <u>who does not</u> take up <u>his</u> <u>cross and</u> follow <u>after me</u> is not worthy of <u>me</u>."	[27]Whoever <u>does not</u> carry <u>his</u> own <u>cross and</u> come <u>after me</u> cannot be <u>my</u> disciple."

Matthew 18:15, 21–22	Luke 17:3–4
	[3]"Be on your guard!
[15]"<u>If your brother sins</u> against you, go and point out the fault when you and he are alone.	If your brother sins, rebuke him,
If he listens to you, you have regained your brother."	and if he repents, forgive him.
. . . . [21]Then Peter came and said to him, "Lord, <u>if</u> my brother <u>sins against</u> me, how often should I <u>forgive him</u>? As many as <u>seven times</u>?" [22]Jesus said to him, "I tell you, not <u>seven times</u>, but seventy-seven times."	[4]And <u>if</u> someone <u>sins against</u> you <u>seven times</u> a day, and turns back to you <u>seven times</u> and says, 'I repent,' you must <u>forgive him</u>."

My question again is simple: Is there anything in these passages that compels the conclusion that one has drawn the sayings from the other or that both have drawn from a common literary source?[73] Is the assumption that only literary dependence need or should be invoked not a consequence of our literary default setting, a consequence of our reading such passages through the spectacles or with the blinkers of a mind-set formed by our print-dominated heritage? Ought we not to make the effort to *hear* these traditions as they were shaped and passed down in an oral culture? Ought we not to give more consideration to the likelihood, not to say probability that such *variation* in what is obviously the *same* essential tradition is the result of the flexibility of *oral* performance?[74]

3. *Liturgical tradition.* The two most obvious examples of liturgical tradition are the Lord's Prayer and the words of the Last Supper. By liturgical tradition I mean, of course, traditions that were regularly used in worship in the early churches. That these two traditions were so used is not merely a deduction from the Gospel texts but is confirmed by *Didache* 8.2 and 1 Cor. 11:23–26. How then shall we explain the variations in the traditions of the Lord's Prayer?

Matthew 6:7–15	Luke 11:1–4
[7]"When you are praying, do not heap up empty phrases as the Gentiles do; for they think that they will be heard because of their many words. [8]Do not be like them, for your Father knows what you need before you ask him.	
	[1]He was praying in a certain place, and after he had finished, one of his disciples said to him, "Lord, teach us to pray, as John taught his disciples." [2]He said to them,
[9]Pray then in this way: Our <u>Father</u> who is in heaven, <u>hallowed be your name.</u> [10]<u>Your kingdom come.</u>	"When you pray, say: <u>Father,</u> <u>hallowed be your name. Your kingdom come.</u>

73. My distinguished predecessor, C. K. Barrett, was asking the same question sixty years ago in his "Q: A Re-examination," *ExpTim* 54 (1942–43): 320–23.

74. As Streeter recognized (*Four Gospels*, 184–86, 229).

Matthew 6:7–15	Luke 11:1–4
Your will be done, on earth as it is in heaven. [11]Give us today our daily bread. [12]And forgive us our debts, as we also have forgiven our debtors. [13]And do not bring us to the time of trial, but rescue us from the evil one. [14]For if you forgive others their trespasses, your heavenly Father will also forgive you; [15]but if you do not forgive others, neither will your Father forgive your trespasses."	[3]Give us each day our daily bread. [4]And forgive us our sins, for we ourselves also forgive everyone indebted to us. And do not bring us to the time of trial."

So too, how shall we explain the variations in the traditions of the Last Supper, as between the Matthew/Mark version on the one hand and the Luke/Paul version on the other?

Matthew 26:26–29	Mark 14:22–25
[26]While they were eating, Jesus took a loaf of bread, and after blessing it he broke it, giving it to the disciples, and said, "Take, eat; this is my body." [27]Then he took a cup, and after giving thanks he gave it to them, saying, "Drink from it, all of you; [28]for this is my blood of the covenant, which is poured out for many for the forgiveness of sins. [29]I tell you, from now on I will not drink of this fruit of the vine until that day when I drink it new with you in the kingdom of my Father."	[22]While they were eating, he took a loaf of bread, and after blessing it he broke it, gave it to them, and said, "Take; this is my body." [23]Then he took a cup, and after giving thanks he gave it to them, and all of them drank from it. [24]He said to them, "This is my blood of the covenant, which is poured out on behalf of many. [25]Truly I tell you, no more will I drink of the fruit of the vine until that day when I drink it new in the kingdom of God."

Luke 22:17–20	1 Corinthians 11:23–26
[17]Then he took a cup, and after giving thanks he said, "Take this and divide it among yourselves; [18]for I tell you that from now on I will not drink of the fruit of the vine until the kingdom of God comes."	

Luke 22:17–20	1 Corinthians 11:23–26
	[23]For I received from the Lord what I also handed on to you, that the Lord Jesus on the night when he was betrayed
[19]Then he took a loaf of bread, and when he had given thanks, he broke it and	took a loaf of bread, [24]and when he had given thanks, he broke it and
gave it to them, saying,	said,
"This is my body,	"This is my body
which is given for you. Do this in remembrance of me."	which is for you. Do this in remembrance of me."
[20]Also the cup likewise after supper, saying, "This cup is the new covenant in my blood which is poured out for you."	[25]Likewise also the cup after supper, saying, "This cup is the new covenant in my blood.
	Do this, as often as you drink it, in remembrance of me." [26]For as often as you eat this bread and drink the cup, you proclaim the Lord's death until he comes.

What kind of failure in historical imagination could even suggest to us that Matthew, say, only knew the Lord's Prayer because he read it in Q?[75] Or that Luke only knew the words of the Last Supper because he found them in Mark? The alternative explanation positively cries out for consideration: that these were living traditions, living because they were used in regular church assemblies; that even though liturgical tradition tends to be more stable than other oral tradition, nevertheless, as is

75. Contrast D. E. Oakman, "The Lord's Prayer in Social Perspective," in *Authenticating of the Words of Jesus*, ed. B. Chilton and C. A. Evans (Leiden: Brill, 1999), 137–86: "The differences in form are best accounted for by differing scribal traditions and interests" (151–52); with the sounder judgment of H. D. Betz, *The Sermon on the Mount*, Hermeneia (Minneapolis: Fortress, 1995), 370–71: "It is characteristic of liturgical material in general that textual fixation occurs at a later stage in the transmission of these texts, while in the oral stage variability within limits is the rule. These characteristics also apply to the Lord's Prayer. The three recensions, therefore, represent variations of the prayer in the oral tradition. . . . There was never only *one original written* Lord's Prayer. . . . The oral tradition continued to exert an influence on the written text of the New Testament well into later times" (370). Goulder, "The Composition of the Lord's Prayer," *Journal of Theological Studies* 14 (1963): 32–45, argues that the prayer was written by Matthew from hints found in Mark, and that Luke was dependent on Matthew's version.

common with oral tradition, it adapted in wording to the usage of different churches—as the Lord's Prayer still adapts in different traditions today. Such liturgical traditions are special examples of oral tradition and oral transmission, but they reflect the character of oral communities far more closely than do explanations dependent solely on the literary paradigm.

4. *Stylistic features.* There are several stylistic features characteristic of oral tradition: for example, parataxis,[76] rhythmic speech,[77] repetition,[78] multiple existence, and variation.[79] This is not to say, I repeat, that such features are *distinctive* of oral tradition; the written document, Mark, provides one of the best examples of parataxis. However, the question once again arises whether the tradition retold by Mark is retold *in oral mode*, rather than as a distinctively literary exercise[80]—a question once again of how we envisage the character of the tradition used by Mark, as also how we envisage Mark's use of it.

One of the best-attested characteristics of oral tradition is the *pattern of threes*—stories built on three episodes or illustrations. Such patterning positively invites the oral performer to vary the examples or episodes at his own whim, often quite spontaneously within the performance itself. There are some good examples of this feature within the Jesus tradition. I cite two, focusing only on the section where the pattern of threes is followed. First, Matt. 22:5–6//Luke 14:18–20, the excuses made by those invited to the great supper or royal wedding banquet; note again how little verbal agreement there is between them.[81]

76. "One law of narrative in oral poetry, noted by specialists, takes the form of parataxis: the language is additive, as image is connected to image by 'and' rather than subordinated in some thoughtful relationship" (Havelock, *Muse*, 76).

77. Havelock, *Muse*, 70–71. Here the examples from the Jesus tradition produced by J. Jeremias, *New Testament Theology*, part 1, *The Proclamation of Jesus* (London: SCM, 1971), are very much to the point (20–27).

78. Achtemeier, "*Omne verbum sonat*," 23–24.

79. See above, n57.

80. See particularly J. Dewey, "Oral Methods of Structuring Narrative in Mark," *Interpretation* 43 (1989): 32–44; also "The Gospel of Mark as an Oral-Aural Event: Implications for Interpretation," in *The New Literary Criticism and the New Testament*, ed. E. S. Malbon and E. V. McKnight, JSNTSup 109 (Sheffield: Sheffield Academic Press, 1994), 145–63; Horsley, *Hearing the Whole Story*, ch. 3.

81. Note that in *Gospel of Thomas* 64, the performance variation runs to four different excuses.

Matthew 22:1–10	Luke 14:15–24
¹Once more Jesus spoke to them in parables, saying: ²"The kingdom of heaven may be compared to a king who gave a wedding banquet for his son. ³He sent his slaves to call those who had been invited to the wedding banquet, but they would not come. ⁴Again he sent other slaves, saying, 'Tell those who have been invited: Look, I have prepared my dinner, my oxen and my fat calves have been slaughtered, and everything is ready; come to the wedding banquet.' ⁵But they made light of it and went away, one to his *farm*, another to his business, ⁶while the rest seized his slaves, mistreated them, and killed them. ⁷The king was angered. He sent his troops, destroyed those murderers, and burned their city. ⁸Then he said to his slaves, 'The wedding is ready, but those invited were not worthy. ⁹Go therefore into the streets, and invite everyone you find to the wedding banquet.'	¹⁵One of the dinner guests, on hearing this, said to him, "Blessed is anyone who will eat bread in the kingdom of God!" ¹⁶Then Jesus said to him, "A certain person gave a great dinner and invited many. ¹⁷At the time for the dinner he sent his slave to say to those who had been invited, 'Come; for it is now prepared.' ¹⁸But they all alike began to make excuses. The first said to him, 'I have bought a *farm*, and I must go out and see it; please accept my regrets.' ¹⁹Another said, 'I have bought five yoke of oxen, and I am going to try them out; please accept my regrets.' ²⁰Another said, 'I have married a wife, and therefore I cannot come.' ²¹So the slave returned and reported this to his master. Then the owner of the house became angry and said to his slave, 'Go out at once into the roads and lanes of the town and bring in the poor, the crippled, the blind, and the lame.'

Matthew 22:1–10	Luke 14:15–24
[10]Those slaves went out into the streets and gathered all whom they found, both good and bad;	
	[22]And the slave said, 'Sir, what you ordered has been done, and there is still room.' [23]Then the master said to the slave, 'Go out into the roads and lanes, and compel them to come in,
so the wedding hall was filled with guests."	so that my house may be full.
	[24]For I tell you, none of those who were invited will taste my dinner.'"

Second, the account of Peter's threefold denial, in Mark 14:66–72 and parallels.

Matthew 26:69–75	Mark 14:66–72	Luke 22:56–62
[69]Now Peter was sitting outside in the courtyard. And a maid	[66]And as Peter was below in the courtyard, one of the maids of the high priest	
		[56]Then a maid,
came up to him,	came; [67]and seeing Peter warming himself, she looked at him,	seeing him as he sat in the light and gazing at him,
and said, "You also were with Jesus the Galilean." [70]But he denied it before them all, saying, "I do not know	and said, "You also were with the Nazarene, Jesus." [68]But he denied it, saying, "I neither know nor understand	said, "This man also was with him." [57]But he denied it, saying, "Woman, I do not know
what you mean." [71]And when he went out to the porch, another maid saw him, and she said to the bystanders, "This man was with Jesus of Nazareth." [72]And again he denied it with an oath, "I do not know the man."	what you mean." And he went out into the gateway. [69]And the maid saw him, and began again to say to the bystanders, "This man is one of them." [70]But again he denied it.	him." [58]And a little later someone else saw him and said, "You also are one of them." But Peter said, "Man, I am not."

Matthew 26:69–75	Mark 14:66–72	Luke 22:56–62
73 After a little while the bystanders came up and said to Peter, "Certainly you are also one of them, for your accent betrays you." 74Then he began to invoke a curse on himself and to swear, "I do not know the man."	And after a little while again the bystanders said to Peter, "Certainly you are one of them; for you are a Galilean." 71But he began to invoke a curse on himself and to swear, "I do not know this man of whom you speak."	59And after an interval of about an hour still another insisted, saying, "Certainly this man also was with him; for he is a Galilean." 60But Peter said, "Man, I do not know what you are saying."
And immediately	72And immediately	And immediately, while he was still speaking,
the cock crowed.	the cock crowed a second time.	the cock crowed.
		61And the Lord turned and looked at Peter.
75And Peter remembered the saying of Jesus, "Before the cock crows, you will deny me three times." And he went out and wept bitterly.	And Peter remembered how Jesus had said to him, "Before the cock crows twice, you will deny me three times." And he broke down and wept.	And Peter remembered the word of the Lord, how he had said to him, "Before the cock crows today, you will deny me three times." 62And he went out and wept bitterly.

In all these cases we see what is characteristic of oral tradition—a combination of fixity and flexibility, of stability and variation. Of course, I repeat yet again, such characteristics are not exclusive to oral tradition. The difference comes in *the way we envisage the traditioning process*. In oral transmission we do not look for an explanation for the diversity in terms (only) of editorial redaction, but in terms of performance variation. The explanation lies as much or more in the character of the tradition than in the interpretative goals of the performer. And we do not look behind the variations for some original (and therefore more authentic) version or source. Rather, we recognize the character of the Jesus tradition as oral tradition, where appropriateness of performance to context is not a departure from authenticity but integral to the tradition's living character.

Had I time, I would extend the exploration to the knowledge of Jesus tradition outside the Gospels. In my judgment, discussion of possible allusions to and use of the Jesus tradition, both within the NT epistles (Paul, James, 1 Peter), within the Apostolic Fathers, and now also within the Nag Hammadi texts, has been seriously flawed by overdependence on the literary paradigm. For if we are indeed talking about largely illiterate communities, dependent on oral tradition and aural knowledge of written documents, then we have to expect *as the rule* that knowledge of the Jesus tradition will have shared the characteristics of oral tradition. That is to say, the historical imagination, liberated from the *literary* default setting and tutored in regard to *oral* culture, can readily envisage communities familiar with *their* oral tradition, able to recognize allusions to Jesus tradition in performances of an apostolic letter written to them, and to fill in "the gaps of indeterminacy" in other performances of that tradition.[82]

The suggestion of a living oral tradition, still continuing after so much of it was written down in various Gospels, carries with it, of course, the possibility that the tradition was significantly modified in its central thrust—that the flexibility overwhelmed the stability, the diversity the continuity. Here we would have to enter the debate about the "authenticity" of the Jesus tradition in the forms that it came to take in documents like the *Gospel of Thomas* and the *Dialogue of the Savior*, not to mention the Gospel of John! That is a debate for another day—in particular, on the criteria by which a form of the tradition was recognized as true to its originating impulse, and on the role of the community in checking the performances of that tradition.[83] Here it must suffice simply to note again that any attempt to resolve

82. I may refer here simply to my earlier attempts to develop this theme—"Jesus Tradition in Paul," in *Studying the Historical Jesus: Evaluations of the State of Current Research*, ed. B. Chilton and C. A. Evans (Leiden: Brill, 1994), 155–78, particularly 176–78; also Dunn, *The Theology of Paul the Apostle* (Grand Rapids: Eerdmans; Edinburgh: Clark, 1998), 651–53.

83. At this point I would wish to take issue with a central thrust of Koester's magisterial contribution, *Ancient Christian Gospels*.

the issue purely in terms of literary dependence, or of the literary concept of the "original" form of the tradition, is hardly likely to prove satisfactory in the long run. Unless we take seriously the oral character of the early transmission of the Jesus tradition, we are always going to be in the position of one who attempts to describe a horse as a wheelless automobile, with the misperception of what we are trying to describe as the unavoidable outcome.

Conclusions and Corollaries

I believe we are confronted with a stark alternative: either we continue to operate within the literary paradigm and allow it to determine the way we envisage the earliest churches, their knowledge of the Jesus tradition, and their use of it; or we deliberately alter that default setting and attempt consciously to envisage a world strange to us, a world of rampant illiteracy, a world where information was communicated orally, a world where knowledge in the vast majority of cases came from hearing rather than from reading. There is room for compromise on this alternative, but not as much as we have simply assumed. For if we allow that the Jesus tradition as it has come down to us consists to any extent of various performances, frozen in writing to be sure, but no less in the first instance *performances*, rather than edited versions of some "original," then our basic methodologies of source and form and redaction criticism become increasingly speculative in their application and uncertain in their outcome.

Consider what corollaries we are loaded with when we opt for exclusive or over-dependence on the literary paradigm. For no hypothesis is more vulnerable to reductio ad absurdum than the hypothesis of an exclusively literary explanation for the Synoptic tradition. Was there no Jesus tradition known and used and circulated before Mark (or Q) wrote it down? Of course there was. Was the tradition wholly inert until Mark gave it life by writing it down? Of course not. Did Mark have to seek out aging apostles or rummage for scraps in boxes hidden away in various elders' houses in order to gather unknown, unused tradition and set it out in writing? Of course not. Was the tradition gathered by Mark known only to Mark's church or circle of congregations? Surely not. And once Mark had gathered the tradition into his Gospel, did that mean that the tradition ceased to be oral? Of course not. Or again, when Matthew received Mark's Gospel, are we to assume that this was the first time Matthew or his church(es) had come across this tradition? Of course not. What is the alternative? The alternative is to recognize that in an oral culture, tradition—oral tradition—is *communal memory*. A group's tradition is the means by which the group affirms and celebrates what is important about its origins and about its past. So the alternative is to envisage little groups of disciples and sympathizers, their identity as a group given by their shared response to Jesus himself or to one of his disciples/apostles—little groups who met regularly to share the memories and the traditions that bound them together, for elders or teachers to tell again stories of Jesus and to expound afresh and elaborate his teachings.

Of course, Good Friday and Easter made a difference. They brought illumination to many features of the earlier tradition. They became integral to the tradition and often more important than the earlier tradition. Easter faith became the context in which the tradition was performed. I do not question that for a moment. But the fact remains that much if not most of the pre-Easter tradition retained its pre-Easter content and perspective, and various clear indications of its Galilean provenance.[84] The very features that Q specialists read as evidence of a *post*-Easter Galilean community that knew nothing of the passion narrative are much more naturally read as evidence of Jesus' *own pre*-passion *Galilean* mission. That character was already impressed in and on the Jesus tradition as it was orally circulated already during the mission of Jesus.

And of course the transition from village to city, and from Aramaic to Greek, introduced still further factors influencing the preaching, telling, and performance of the Jesus tradition. But here again, the preservation of that Galilean, pre-passion character of so much of the tradition, now in Greek, and circulating in ever-widening circles as new churches were estab-

---

84. See particularly H. Schürmann, "Die vorösterlichen Anfänge der Logientradition: Versuch eines formgeschichtlichen Zugangs zum Leben Jesu," in *Der historische Jesus und der kerygmatische Christus*, ed. H. Ristow and K. Matthiae (Berlin: Evangelische Verlag, 1961), 342–70; also idem, *Jesus: Gestalt und Geheimnis* (Paderborn: Bonifatius, 1994), 85–104, 380–97.

lished, indicates that it was the *same* tradition that was being thus circulated and used. The essential character of that tradition was being maintained in and through the diversity of its performances.

On this model that I ask you to envisage, we need not assume that *Mark* wrote down all the tradition known to him. We can envisage quite readily that the tradition he drew upon continued to circulate in oral communication and was known more widely than the Gospel itself. Also, we can allow that Mark's Gospel itself functioned for many as itself a kind of oral performance,[85] known only by hearing, and recalled on the basis of that hearing. We can assume that *Matthew* knew at least many of the traditions written down by Mark, and knew the tradition almost certainly in different versions, in accordance with the nature of oral tradition. Also, we can assume that in various instances Matthew probably preferred the version of the tradition that he already knew, rather than Mark's. The same with Luke.

The corollaries regarding Q are of greater consequence, particularly in the light of the latest attempt to recover the text of Q.[86] For if much of the shared Matthew and Luke material attests *oral* dependency rather than *literary* dependency, then *the attempt to define the complete scope and limits of Q is doomed to failure.* It is not simply that by definition of "Q" (material common to Matthew and Luke) we cannot know its scope and limits, since wherever Matthew or Luke decided not to use "Q" we do not have "Q"![87] It is rather that the material common to Matthew and Luke itself attests the pervasiveness of *oral* Jesus tradition precisely in its *variability*, as well as whatever of that material had already become more fixed in writing (as Q).[88]

85. See again n80, above.

86. J. M. Robinson et al., eds., *The Critical Edition of Q* (Minneapolis: Fortress; Leuven: Peeters, 2000).

87. The spate of recent work on Q has provoked several vigorous responses, particularly C. S. Rodd, "The End of the Theology of Q?" *ExpTim* 113 (2001–2): 5–12; and Goodacre, *Case against Q.* The case *against* Q is only as strong as it is because the case *for* Q has been overstated.

88. Cf. F. G. Downing, "Word-Processing in the Ancient World: The Social Production and Performance of Q," *Journal for the Study of the New Testament* 64 (1996): 29–48, reprinted in his *Doing Things with Words in the First Christian Century*, JSNTSup 200 (Sheffield: Sheffield Academic Press, 2000), 75–94, especially 92–93.

I fully appreciate that the consequences of altering the default setting so abruptly are extensive. When we abandon the hypothesis of exclusive literary dependence, *we will simply be unable to trace the tradition-history of various sayings and accounts so confidently.* The unknown factors and variations so characteristic of oral tradition put the tradition-history or, better, performance-history beyond reach. The model of linear development, layer upon layer, edition following edition, is no longer appropriate.

Let me press the point more strongly. In recognizing the oral character of the early Jesus tradition, we have to give up the idea of a *single original form* from which all other versions of the tradition are to be derived, as though the "authenticity" of a version depended on our ability to trace it back to that original. In so saying, again, I do *not* mean that it is impossible to envisage or speak of the *originating impact* of Jesus himself. Quite the contrary. What I mean is that from the first the original impact was itself *diverse* in character. What I mean is that the form of the tradition itself was from the first *multi*form. This also means that *variation in tradition does not of itself either indicate contradiction or denote editorial manipulation.* Variation is simply the hallmark of oral tradition, how the Jesus tradition functioned.

In consequence also, we see how unrealistic is the suggestion that we can define the character of a community from the character of the documents they held in their possession. And the suggestion that the character of a community can be restricted to the character of a single document (for example, the Q community) becomes little short of ludicrous. For if the Jesus tradition was relatively widespread among churches in oral form and if indeed the Jesus tradition formed a kind of network linking the churches, as apostles, prophets, and others moved among them, then there is no good reason to limit the Jesus tradition known to individual churches to a certain kind of tradition or a particular written version of some of that tradition.

Confronted by the greater uncertainty thereby implied, some may be tempted to invoke Occam's razor: Why multiply unknown factors when a simple two-document hypothesis with redaction can cover every eventuality?[89] The answer is that the simplicity

89. But it is a double-edged razor, since both Farmer (*Synoptic Problem*, 203) and Goodacre (*Case against Q*, 18, 77) can use it to excise one of "the

envisaged is far from simple, since it has to postulate editorial ingenuity of tremendous complexity and sophistication. Much more simple in fact is the inference that the variations within the Synoptic tradition reflect more closely the kind of variations that were common in the performance traditions of the early churches. Again I stress that it need not be an either-or matter. I am not arguing for one against the other; I am arguing for both.[90]

There is much more to be said about the way the Jesus tradition was used in performance by apostles and teachers. For example, I have already noted how Lord's observation that "oral traditional composers think in terms of blocks and series of blocks of tradition" correlates well with the various groupings or clusters of pericopes evident in the Synoptic tradition.[91] We need not assume, as the early form critics did, that before the written-down stage, the tradition was used only in small, individual units.[92] And we should reexamine the old suggestion of C. H. Dodd, that already in the prewritten (oral only) Gospel stage we can detect what we might call a narrative- or kerygma-sequencing of tradition.[93] For the connectedness of the passion narrative still attests some such concern, as does the fact that Mark and Q both reflect a common intuition (practice?) of beginning their rehearsal of the Jesus tradition with John the Baptist.[94] Just as elsewhere it seems to be "taken-for-granted and familiar" that a period of Jesus' mission in Capernaum preceded his return to Nazareth (Luke 4:23), and that the mission of the Twelve was a consequence of time spent with Jesus (made explicit in Mark 3:14), and so on. Thus

two documents" (Q). It is a fallacy to assume that elegance of solution can be achieved simply by restricting the range of options that the character of the evidence invites.

90. Streeter had already noted the danger of imposing an oversimplified solution on more complex data (*Four Gospels*, 229).

91. Above, nn53–54.

92. Pace Funk and Hoover (n20, above), who would regard their observation as form-critical orthodoxy.

93. C. H. Dodd, "The Framework of the Gospel Narrative," *New Testament Studies* (Manchester: Manchester University Press, 1953), 1–11. See further also Reicke, *Roots*; S. Hultgren, *Narrative Elements in the Double Tradition: A Study of Their Place within the Framework of the Gospel Narrative*, Beihefte zur Zeitschrift für die neutestamentliche Wissenschaft 113 (Berlin: de Gruyter, 2002).

94. See also N. T. Wright, *The New Testament and the People of God* (London: SPCK, 1992), 442; Schröter, *Erinnerung*, 439–51.

the sequencing of the centurion's servant after the collection of Jesus' teaching (Sermon on Mount/Plain), which provides a decisive argument for the inclusion of the centurion's servant in Q (Matt. 7:28; 8:5–13//Luke 7:1–10), may after all be better explained as a recurring feature of the various performances of the Jesus tradition in more than one community.[95]

A fuller study of the Jesus tradition as oral tradition would also need to examine more closely what balance between stability and variation, between fixity and flexibility, was actually maintained, what it means to speak of the *same* tradition being maintained through the diversity of oral performance, and how Jesus was actually remembered in and by those earliest disciple groups. I have attempted to press further in this direction in my study *Jesus Remembered*. In the present essay, it has been a sufficient challenge to attempt to persuade you of the need to alter our inherited literary default setting, which (in my judgment) has contorted the way we envisage the early transmission of the Jesus tradition.

Perhaps the point most to be emphasized in conclusion is that to recognize the character of the Jesus tradition as oral tradition is to recognize its character also as *living* tradition. The Jesus tradition was not at first a written text, to be read by individuals in the solitude of their studies, capable of fine literary analysis and redaction. It was not carried around like a sacred relic fixed in written form. It was living tradition, lived-in-and-through tradition. It was not so much kept as used, not so much preserved as performed, not so much read as heard. To treat it as a lifeless artifact, suitable for clinical dissection, is to lose it. Its variability, the oral principle of "variation within the same," is not a sign of degeneration or corruption. Rather, it puts us directly in touch with the tradition in its living character, as it was heard in the earliest Christian groups and churches, and can still be heard and responded to today.

In short, to alter the default setting is to refuse to treat the Jesus tradition first and only as a written text, and to insist on the importance of *hearing* it, of hearing it as it was heard in the beginning, and of hearing it also as a tradition that still lives and still demands response from its hearers as it did from the beginning.

95. This in response to Goodacre, *Case against Q*, 172n6.

Scripture Index

127

Subject Index

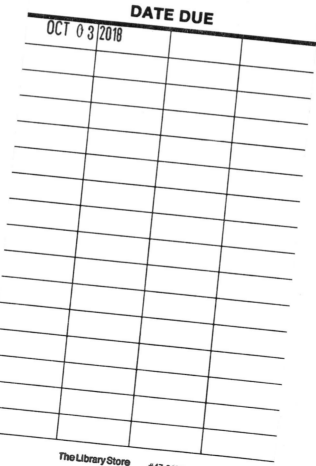